HOW CAN I UNDERSTAND MY CHILD?

Know how through their

Western and Chinese birth signs

Aries and the 12 Chinese Astrological Signs

ISBN: 978-0-9909751-6-8

Table of Contents

PRAISE FOR THE BOOK

"Once Luis had given me the characteristics of my daughter, little by little I saw that what he had written was not only true, but this has helped me better understand my daughter. It has allowed me to see her as a person in her own right. Thank you Luis for being so generous in sharing your knowledge with us." **Adriana S.**

"After Luis gave me the characteristics of my three children, at first I was surprised, then I was interested, and finally I was grateful. For his detailed descriptions helped me to understand why and how my children developed throughout their youth. My children too learned how best to use their potential, plus how best to control their weaknesses. I never thought astrology could help the understanding of children in such a way." **Paloma S.**

"Since Luis gave me the characteristics of my three boys, as time has passed most of what he stated has come true. Even to predict their future development as adults. I did not realize the importance of birth signs in a child's potential. I am forever grateful of Luis' contribution towards my children's education." **Susana J.**"

I asked Luis to write about my eldest grandson who was in his final year of school. What Luis wrote was very amazingly realistic and revealing. Both my grandson and his parents appreciated this input very much at such a vulnerable and life changing time for my grandson. We wish you well with this book that will no doubt help many struggling parents." **Luisa T.**

ABOUT THE AUTHOR

Born in Gibraltar and diagnosed with dyslexia as a child, Luis Proetta Gonzalez went on to graduate with distinction from London University's St. Mary's Teaching College and become a life-long educator. He was an active school teacher for twenty-five years in a variety of different classrooms at the Cardinal Wiseman Catholic School in Greenford, London and the Bishop Fitzgerald School in Gibraltar. Next, Luis spent thirty-five years as an independent, self-made Headmaster at Calpe International College, an all-age comprehensive school in southern Spain distinguished for pioneering educational excellence, particularly for children with learning difficulties. His educational philosophy is to teach children as individuals and present subjects as living information for one's own betterment as well as academic achievement.

During his years as an educator, Luis came to understand there are forces that influence the way we behave aside from genetic influences and one's upbringing. This knowledge led him to run a seven year astrological experiment in his art department in which he studied the work produced by every child and measured it against their Western Sun Sign and their Eastern Personality Sign based on the Chinese Twelve Year Personality Zodiac. The results proved these influences characterize who a person is, the way they see things, how they behave and how they are interwoven to produce 144 individual types of children.

DEDICATION

For my soul mate, Astrid Plagge, who suggested I write a book
instead of building another school some eleven years ago.

And my soul sister, Barbara Lynn, who has turned
my enthusiastic jumble into readable text.

Without them this book would not exist.

FOREWORD

Dear reader, these character analyses aim to describe the behavior of children from very young to reaching their late teenage years. I have tended to describe the male's type of behaviors, rather than the female's (the reasons for this for later.) So this is why I am referring to him and not her in these tight descriptions. I do however mention sometimes how a girl could behave when necessary to describe how her behavior can be different to that of a boy. An example of this would be the female tigress, who is not at all shy or reserved when she is after what she wants.

But before I go any further I have to admit I can only be 80% correct (at most) in my descriptions. This is because the other 20% of the personality is made up of personal influences that include the following:

Genetic background, which contributes to looks and general attitude towards life.

The conditions he/she is subjected to during the early years (up to three years old), which is hardwiring that affects the automatic subconscious reactions to certain stimuli.

And that I believe everyone has a unique soul or higher self that has a karmic or personal journey to complete on this earth which affects the personality.

Now to explain the reasons for this choice of gender, and it is not because I prefer the male domination over the sexes, but because the 'normal' male behaviors are more open and easier to notice and therefore to understand. I believe the female personality to generally be more subdued and not so 'up front,' as that of most males.

However, the traits described here are the same for both sexes, but their hardwiring in their future development, because of their different genetic makeup plus their different type of upbringing, can and does make a slight difference in their overall development, and this will be noticed in their final personality portrait.

At times I have been accused that these descriptions tend to highlight the more negative habits of the personal character in question. Certainly this personality portrait is not meant to be damming or confronting. I do this because I try to describe the traits and attitudes which perhaps parents don't want to talk about, don't want to acknowledge, or hide from. Because it is better to be aware and accept these traits, rather than endure continuous upset and live with the hope that one day all the difficult traits will be put right as the child matures. Because I do not share this philosophy I therefore point out the weaker traits, as well as the more positive ones, with the hope that by being honest the 'subject in question' will try to mend his ways.

So by describing the annoying traits of each personality along with their remedy, I hope to help parents and teachers to understand why each individual character behaves the way he/she does, and then suggest ways of easing the conflicting situation.

Secondly, if I was to stress only the good traits of each character, to please the readers, what good would it do when the parents are faced with anti-social behavior? With no idea of why it is happening or what to do about it! I therefore believe that I have to describe the negative behavior first and then what to do about it.

As a person I prefer to be realistic and candid, with a flair for showmanship, as I am a simple Virgo/Rooster. And the version I give of each personality I can 'see' through my own hardwiring, with 80+ years of life experience, 60 of them as a teacher and headmaster. Such was my desire to prove that my version of education was the best that in 1971 I opened my own school. As Headmaster I was able to ensure that the focus was placed on treating each child as an individual, and preparing them for LIFE, and not just to pass exams.

It is with pride that I remember that each daily assembly would finish with the children shouting out the school's motto 'I will do my very best to day` and I would say `Let God do the rest.' I retired from full-time teaching in 2004 and passed the reins of the school to my son, who continues to maintain the same tradition.

And I am very happy to state that I am still remembered today by many of my pupils as one of the best teachers and headmasters they ever had. So if at times I tend to dictate my words, and my keen thoughts are confronting, it's all because it is a matter of habit and hard core experience. I have dealt with and studied thousands of students and hundreds of teachers and parents. Plus I am by nature a very observant person, with a good memory, which is all part of my own survival skills because being part dyslexic, I have the ability to take calculated risks which others may hesitate to take, but in my case have ended up being very successful.

THE CHINESE ASTROLOGICAL YEAR CHART

The Chinese astrological chart designates an animal and its reputed attributes to each year in a repeating 12-year cycle. As with many ancient traditions the origins of the stories vary, however my belief is based on the ancient story of the Great Race which was held to determine which animals would be placed in the chart for eternity.

It is a little known fact that the Chinese astrological personality chart was written 2,000 years before the Byzantine twelve sun signs, more commonly known as the Western zodiac.

The Chinese New Year follows the lunar calendar with the date being the new moon on the first day of the year in the traditional Chinese calendar. Because of this, Chinese New Year is never on January 1st, and each new year will fall on a date between January 21st and February 20th. For those people born between these dates, I recommend going online and verifying your animal sign.

Rat
1960, 1972, 1984,
1996, 2008, 2020

Ox
1961, 1973, 1985,
1997, 2009, 2021

Tiger
1962, 1974, 1986,
1998, 2010, 2022

Cat
1963, 1975, 1987,
1999, 2011, 2023

Dragon
1964, 1976, 1988,
2000, 2012, 2024

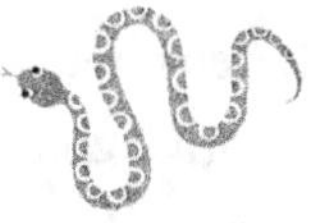

Snake
1965, 1977, 1989,
2001, 2013, 2025

Horse
1966, 1978, 1990,
2002, 2014, 2026

Goat
1967, 1979, 1991,
2003, 2015, 2027

Monkey
1968, 1980, 1992,
2004, 2016, 2028

Rooster
1969, 1981, 1993,
2005, 2017, 2029

Dog
1970, 1982, 1994,
2006, 2018, 2030

Pig
1971, 1983, 1995,
2007, 2019, 2031

NOTE TO THE READER

My purpose in writing this book is to provide comprehensive information that parents and educators can use to help children understand themselves and thereby gain the ability to control and utilize their inborn positive and negative characteristics. Doing so leads children on a path of self-discovery and helps them overcome self-doubts, develop their natural abilities, improve social standing and achieve balance in their life; for at the base of all human needs is the prerequisite of developing a balanced relationship with oneself. Only then can we develop solid relationships with others.

So after reading about a child's double astrological characteristics, this youth will gain the information which will certainly help him/her to mature into adulthood. And by using this new data, he will better understand himself. Through the discovery of his inborn traits, and the knowledge that these can become his biggest assets, he will gain in his self-confidence and realize his own worth.

However, before diving into the double birth sign that interests you, my recommendation is that you start by reading the section on the Aries Sun Sign. Whilst the positive and negative traits of Aries are the same for each of the Chinese Personality Signs, it serves to give a much more rounded description of the child.

At the end of each double birth sign's description I have include a summary of their characteristics and behaviour: the good, and not so good, with recommendations on how to handle the child if they are misbehaving.

And finally, and to reinforce this child's understanding of themselves, at the end of each of the descriptions is a list of famous personalities who share the same double birth signs. I have chosen these people because their life stories encapsulate the characteristics and traits of the combined Sun Sign and Chinese Personality.

Reading about some of these personalities should interest and even motivate the child to follow in their footsteps. By noting how the characteristics of the double birth signs don't change through time, he would discover that all his heroes would have had to use all their natural talents to achieve great deeds. Some in the intellectual world, others in their sporting activities, but all would have had to overcome personal difficulties by using their self-discipline, determination and self-belief, and of course with lots of hard work, and thereby hopefully encouraging them to be proud to have been born at the right time of the month and year, and to have been endowed with so many positive talents and abilities.

UNDERSTANDING THE ARIES SUN SIGN:

For those who are not familiar with the astrological sign of Aries it is important to know that it is the first of our Western Sun Signs and as the first it can be seen as the pioneer of all the other eleven birth signs which follow.

In a nut shell, this birth sign is the basic leader who looks after himself, his family and those close to him. He can be kind with those he loves and protects, but hard with those he believes can stop him from doing what he wants. He can show just how selfish he can be by the way he acts and reacts in situations where he thinks he is losing control. For him, what is most important is to be in charge of what is going on around him.

He is a better friend than an enemy, though more mature birth signs can see him coming from afar and can avoid any problems with him. But though he can be seen as simple, he is cunning enough to put himself in the lead in most situations. His best trait is that he is honest and hardworking, and will face up to most challenges that he can understand.

His control over his emotions can be compared to that of an overgrown child, so he can become stubborn or angry when he cannot achieve what he wants or needs. And neither will he stop trying to achieve his targets by using any tool he has at hand. If then despite trying hard he fails, he will just leave and look for something else which he can dominate. However, one can always depend on him to be brave in situations of panic, when other more sensitive people would fold, he will stand up and be counted.

THE POSITIVE TRAITS OF ARIES:

His courage as the basic hunter who, without prompting, will provide for himself and his family all the necessary goods needed to live comfortably. And while he is young, this attitude is backed by a direct drive to achieve his ends as easily as possible, not really minding how he gets what he wants. For to provide for his needs he will follow his basic instincts so he always comes-out-on-top of any situation, never shying from drastic-action if it is needed. And to achieve this he will use his basic talents for enterprise and innovation to make sure he survives any unforeseen circumstances while out hunting. But his selfish behaviors are mostly defended by his disarming attitude, which can melt anyone's heart! Even when he is being naughty, as he will always have a good excuse for being single-minded.

This individualistic pioneering attitude is basic to his dealings with others, for he sees no reason why others do not behave like he does or do the things he does. His motto as an Aries is, 'I will defend myself and provide for my family,' or the other way round. For this Aries sign is the original hunter type personality, quick to take advantage of any situation for his own personal gain. And he will see no reason for not being single-minded to achieve his ends. I also have to add that this sign is seen as the most primitive in Western Astrology, being the first of our Zodiac Sun Signs.

And to back up this statement I can continue with the following. Because this Aries personality has to live in a community, he has learned to hide his direct ways by becoming very friendly and affable, but if anyone tries to get the better of him he will turn aggressive in his self-defense.

And as for his defense, he will use whatever tactic, tool or weapon he has at hand. And if he fails in his quest he will not give up, for he believes in the motto, 'if you fail you just try again and again.' What has to be admired in this child's character is his courage, as he tries his best to succeed, and then the acceptance that when he has not done so, he will be tolerant with himself, happily, without emotional resentments. But he will cover this disappointment by becoming a sterner leader and try even harder to become more inventive in his methods to overtake those who he considers are better than him.

THE NEGATIVE TRAITS OF ARIES:

Aries suffers from his need to dominate others, who he thinks might interfere with his wishes. This despotic attitude leads him to become excessive in his behaviors, as he goes around overlooking what is happening within his circle of activities. For he feels, that he has to show that he is important to become the natural leader of any group he is in. And he will back this attitude with a show of his ostentatious bravado. Plus, he will demonstrate this aggressive show with his claim that he can get what he wants, unhindered by others, even if they stand in his way. Simply because in his aggressive actions he can be cunning and willful. Added to this he is full of pretense, to show his prowess, as he tries to intimidate others, who might deny his wishes by using his sheer ferocity.

However the singularity of this character is his naivety can become his strength as well as his downfall. For once it has been discovered that he can at times be just hot air, his cover is blown, and he will have to rethink his defensive tactics. I believe our Astrologers chose this first character description well, for we see the Aries as the basic hunter/warrior who uses all his simple strategies during the hunt to achieve what he wants. Though most of the time this Aries will use the act of pretense as his first tactic to fool his adversary into believing he is smarter than he is. In fact, many animals use this type of tactic as a form of attack or self-defense, only they are not as charming as this child/youth.

CHAPTER 1

ARIES/RAT

THE ARIES/RAT PERSONALITY

The combination of Aries and the Rat year produces a child who is full of fun and energy, and who is not normally naughty or unruly, but loves to be active. For in his busy mind he expects to be amused by his parents, or else he will find ways to amuse himself, though not always in the way his parents or teachers would have him behave. The Aries/ Rat personality is strong and direct, but also naïve and smart, certainly when it comes to looking after himself (and those he loves). At home and at school an Aries/Rat will call attention to himself by his sheer energy and ability to be at the center of any action. His ability to lead will soon become obvious, as he will be the first one to dare to try any new game introduced by his parents or teachers. Because he was born to be adventurous, this trait will stimulate him into an eagerness to test himself with any new adventure.

This means that his love and hate emotions will be direct in showing themselves, so he will need firm handling or else he will take over the reins in any open, unorganized situation. Parents with a child born as an Aries/Rat should be prepared to have a fireball in the family. But with simple and firm directions, this child should prove easy enough to rear. Because the Aries is basic in his needs and the Rat is the world's survivor, this merger has the potential of producing a basic personality who is simple, yet a powerful human being with open, strong characteristics.

Aries, as we all know, is the first fire sign and full of pioneering spirit and the original hunter and provider.

There is a story to explain how the Rat was the first animal to be chosen by the Wise Chinese Astrologers to describe their Twelve Year Astrological Personality Cycle. It goes like this: The Chinese God wanted to discover which animal was the smartest and able to survive difficult and awkward situations in the most simple, direct and efficient of ways. So he devised a test to discover the basic intelligence and endurance needed to fulfill these priorities. The winner would then be worthy to be named as the first of the Twelve Yearly Personality Descriptions. Somehow or other the Rat was the first to reach the last obstacle of the race, but he got stuck as he could not swim across a wide river. So he managed to get a lift from the dependable Ox, who helped him across. Then using his guile he cheated the Ox, so that he was able to win the race and in doing so demonstrated his audacity and power to achieve what is considered almost impossible.

I believe this story was fashioned by the Wise Chinese Astrologers to add credence to their list of 12 animals which they had studied to represent the Twelve Basic Human Prototypes.

THE POSITIVE TRAITS OF THE RAT:

The Rat adds his positive traits of having personal influence over others to seek maximum advantage in whatever situation he finds himself in. This attitude is backed by his basic intellectual skills and his self-discipline to be thrifty with his possessions so that he will always have enough. He will hide this hording attitude for he needs to be sociable to cohabit with many others of his kind, so he develops a certain charisma which helps him achieve what he wants, without the need to fight his corner. What I am describing here is no dirty gutter rat, but rather the healthy rat found in barns in the countryside, looking after his family by using all the survival instincts inborn in his genetic program.

THE NEGATIVE TRAITS OF THE RAT:

The Rat's weakness is to become aggressive if his position in the hierarchy within his family or group is challenged. A Rat will fight to gain control over people or situations which he believes will deter his progress or harm him or his family. This alertness will cause him to be constantly vigilant, so he will show an active nervousness which he will try to conceal through his verbosity. Also, and to protect his status, he will meddle in other peoples' business to discover what they are up to so that he can make plans to protect himself and his interests. As mentioned before, the Rat needs to have a deep well of guile to survive, so its human counterpart is no different.

This means that this personality needs to feel power over others, which he will use as leverage to gain the upper hand in any personal negotiations. For the basic intent in the Rat's thinking is to have enough for his needs, and then to keep the rest safe for later. He could be termed as selfish by some, as hording his possessions and his greed for personal power is not unknown in his practical attitude. Naturally, all these negative traits do not show up all the time, for this Rat is far too cunning to display his negative trends openly. Always wanting to be seen as the good guy, and to avoid being seen as the bad guy, to carry this positive role he will become most helpful, and mean it. So he will become proactive in the most simple and direct of ways. Therefore, I can state that this Rat personality will be known either as a good friend, or a dangerous enemy.

THE EARLY BEHAVIORS OF THE ARIES/RAT CHILD/YOUTH:

Through the merger of these two powerful birth signs, as he matures from a baby to a young adult an Aries/Rat will become a lively, yet demanding young person, who will need to seek attention while at home to make sure he gets what he wants. And he will do this as he investigates and discovers his immediate environment. As an Aries hunter plus a Rat survivor he will charm his way into everyone's heart, or he will simply demand he is well looked after, as he thinks fit. And one way he will do this is by being alert and trying not to cause too many problems at home, because he does not want to be ignored or thought of as just a pest.

For his fear is to be passed over, or that his wishes will not being taken seriously, though he will find ways and means to make sure he is well looked after until he can look after himself. Because to become independent to do as he wishes will be one of his main aims in life. However, until he is able to be free from the care of his parents, this cunning Aries/Rat will abide by what is expected of him. So in a nut shell, this child will be charming while he is satisfied with what he is getting, but demanding if he feels he is missing out from his parents' attention. Particularly when it comes to claiming what he considers are his rights. This selfish attitude of 'me first' he will also show while he is at school and, indeed wherever he goes. For using his self-love inborn instincts he will know just how far he can go to achieve his goals; though he will retreat if he feels he is going to lose out by becoming too aggressive. Nevertheless, being taken for granted as a personality is not his idea of being accepted for who he is. At no time will he want to be seen as just another ordinary child/youth seeking adult attention, because he will not act like one.

THE TACTICS USED BY THIS ARIES/RAT TO BE NOTICED:

To be different, he will show his raw cunning in the way he acts at home. An Aries/Rat will gauge how best to behave to reap the most rewards from those adults around him. He will make use of his double inborn instincts to attack or retreat in order to survive. In fact, I will go as far as to say that he will have a big say on how he is looked after by those adults who are caring for him. He will judge when it is convenient for him to be picked up or laid down, and certainly when he is fed. If he feels he is being well taken care of he will not cause any trouble. Most of all he will enjoy being made a fuss of, but not too much to bother him as he will just cry, even kick out when he gets angry. So one can say that he is the basic child who knows what he wants from the start of his early life.

THE ARIES/RAT AS THE FIRST BORN:

Being the first born would be his best place, for he would love to take charge of his siblings and look after them (in a mature, fatherly way). His siblings would have to obey him or else, particularly when they are young, and in his mind defenseless. But by and large he would be loving and protective towards them with just a bit of meddling in their personal affairs, for their own good. But as their protector, he will try to discover and improve his abilities on how best to get his own way with them without causing them any upsets. These tactics he will follow in preparation for his future self-development as a smart negotiator. Perhaps the most charming aspect of this child/youth is his loyalty towards his family and friends, which he will expect to receive back from them when he needs it.

THE ARIES/RAT AS THE SECOND CHILD:

If this Aries/Rat child is born in the middle or the youngest in his family he would find the ways and means to prove he is independent, strong and loyal towards his family. But unless he is leading his siblings in their group play, he would rather be left alone to do his own thing. For in his self-defensive thinking, to form part of any joint venture where he is not in charge would not suit him as he would find it difficult to trust others to look after his own interests. To be seen as an extra would not be his idea of demonstrating he has strong self-esteem, something he guards jealously. So there is every chance that confrontations with his brothers and sisters will take place if they were to take him for granted as the little one in the family.

THE GENERAL IMAGE OF THE YOUNG ARIES/RAT:

The one important image this Aries/Rat likes to demonstrate is that he is able to be happy and busy by trying to test himself to discover his limitations. I have discovered the best method to control and handle this Aries/Rat personality is to watch over him as he goes through his self-testing actions, even allowing him to get slightly hurt. He has to burn his surplus supply of energy in doing things which might look as if he can get into some minor devilment. All these activities help him discover his potential, though at times he can be plainly silly. But unless he is going to get seriously hurt, allow him his freedom, as he is by nature an inquisitive Aries/Rat who prefers to get hurt, rather than lose face among his peer group. Neither is it a good idea to belittle him when he is leading his peer group, as his main aim will be to look cool and adventurous.

THE ARIES/RAT'S TACTICS TO SHOW HIS BRAVERY:

Though he may want to appear to be brave, funny and independent, this Aries/Rat has a very vulnerable self-image which he guards with extrovert behavior. Because, in his mind, to be seen as a softy because he is too obedient or submissive with adults will destroy his self-made image, an image in which he wants to appear self-reliant, and at times even cheeky. As by being cheeky he will want to enhance his self-esteem, particularly in front of others, as he is playing the part of the potential leader. Though at the same time, this Aries/Rat will not want to overstep the mark of his set boundaries.

In trying to compensate for his self-testing activities, he can then become very friendly, helpful and open in the company of adults. Yet, to safeguard being seen as easily embarrassed, he will hide the fact that he is sensitive to what others may say about him. This internal fear makes him keen to develop a sharp sense of self-love and protection, with the ability of monitoring any strong negative vibrations around him. And due to this subliminal influence, any upset will have a marked effect on his behaviors. Therefore he will need the full support of his parents and teachers when any form of tension prevails, either at home or in his classroom. For knowing that he is being fully protected from harm will calm his fragile survival awareness while he is still young.

THE ARIES/RAT'S BEHAVIOR AT JUNIOR SCHOOL:

During his early youth, until he is about six or seven years old, this Aries/Rat will want to play and be with his friends, for this human contact means more to him than anything his teacher has to say or teach. It is more important for him to learn how to get on with his peers than to learn any academic subject, for instinctively he knows that he can learn these skills later, for he is quite self-confident that he will survive wherever he goes. Also, as a guide for his parents and teachers, any academic work he has to learn has to be presented to him as a challenge, as a test to his personal development. It is likely that he will learn what he's being taught as quickly as everyone else, so this challenge will motivate him not to be left behind, and indirectly not to lose face among his peer group. Though his learning would depend on how much time he is allowed to experiment, or even to show off, added to how much freedom of movement he is afforded in his classroom. Yet he will want to learn as much as he can. He knows that learning facts and manual skills will help him become a freer agent later on. Certainly, as a true astute Aries/Rat, he will know that before he leaves school he needs to have enough basic education to look after himself, as no doubt he will have been told this by his parents and teachers.

THE ARIES/RAT AT SENIOR SCHOOL:

I also have to mention what this young Aries/Rat can get up to regarding his behaviors during his later school life, because it will depend on his upbringing and the type of education he is receiving. Whether it is normal to study and be disciplined in general at home, this Aries/Rat will behave normally at school as he is used to being disciplined to follow a routine. But if at home he is left very much on his own, then the reverse will happen. And it will be the turn of his teachers to instill some form of self-control so that this Aries/Rat can be taught to behave as expected. Now I am not making out that this child/youth is by nature a little wild, but yes, he will need some form of discipline before he can follow any routine which he has not had at home. Beyond this, as a student an Aries/Rat will try to do his best, particularly if his self-love is stimulated. Because to survive he knows that he has to learn, or at least to demonstrate his knowledge. He could become a great all-round student if he is stimulated by being praised by his parents and teachers, both as a family member, and as a student and an athlete.

SUMMARY OF THE ARIES/RAT CHARACTERISTICS AND BEHAVIOR:

☺ Creative, adventurous, courageous, observant, clever, versatile, loyal.

☹ Single-minded, impulsive, aggressive, selfish, arrogant, stubborn, cunning.

IF THIS CHILD IS MISBEHAVING:

He does not mean to be difficult, but will often disregard the rules to suit himself. When he is found out, be straight with him. He needs to be controlled and though he might not like it, he will prefer being nurtured in a strict environment. His idea of being safe is to pretend he knows what to do, and then do what he wants. This tactic, once discovered, has to be challenged and amended. He will comply if his freedom is curtailed rather than being hit in anger.

Depending on how the parent/teacher wants to deal with this child, it can either be the hard way by stopping him from doing something he likes, or spending the time going over the reasons for his naughtiness. Whatever way, this child must understand that he will get into trouble if he crosses the line. The best way to handle this child is to be loving, yet firm and explain that all he needs to do is follow the simple rules. At times there will be no need to negotiate with this clever child, either he does what he is told or he will get punished.

FAMOUS ARIES/RAT PERSONALITIES

Joseph Hayden (31 March 1732): A prolific Austrian composer. He is well recognized and famous worldwide, having a great influence over other composers of his age. His music is as popular today as it was during his life time. He seemed to know what type of music would become popular with the majority of people. Plus he had the power to influence other composers. In fact, he was a true Aries/Rat personality.

Josephine Butler (13 April 1828): An English feminist and social reformer in the Victorian era. She campaigned for women's suffrage, the right of women to better education, the end of coverture in British law, the abolition of child prostitution, and an end to human trafficking of young women and children into European prostitution. She had great powers of communications, which helped her to get people to follow her. A typical Aries/Rat who can follow a dream and make it a reality.

Emile Zola (2 April 1840): a French activist, author and critic. The best-known practitioner of the literary school of naturalism. He was a major figure in the political liberalization of France. Equally important, he became known as one of the great champions of the downtrodden, and he never hesitated to allow his name to be added to any cause. He was nominated for two Nobel Prizes in Literature in 1901 and 1902. His life story is a good prototype to represent the Aries/Rat personality.

Charles Elton (29 March 1900): An English scientist and author. He was interested in animal ecology, having written eight books on the subject. He was known for his studies of invasive organisms, receiving many accolades for his work. He founded and editor for the Journal of Animal Ecology.

Joseph F. Cullman III (9 April 1912): An American and CEO of the Philip Morris Tobacco Company. He defended the industry and the habit of smoking. He was not a tactful personality, for he was almost aggressive when he went on air to deny smoking was hazardous to a person's health. He did not accept the many negative health reports written on the subject, and insisted that they were not valid because he had not found that the evidence given was valid.

Henry Mancini (16 April 1924): An American composer, conductor and arranger, who is best remembered for his film and television scores. Often cited as one of the greatest composers in the history of film, he won four Academy Awards, a Golden Globe, and twenty Grammy Awards, plus a posthumous Grammy Lifetime Achievement Award in 1995. His best known works include the theme to The Pink Panther film series and 'Moon River' from Breakfast at Tiffany's. A true Ares/Rat personality.

Mario Vargas Llosa (28 March 1936): A Peruvian writer, politician, journalist, essayist and winner of the Nobel Prize for Literature in 2010. He is considered one of the leading writers of his age in Latin America and is very well-respected for his innovative work.

Dr. Jiri Grygar (17 April 1936): A Czech astronomer. He holds a PhD in astrophysics and is well known for his research of meteors, comets and variable stars. He has published more than 200 scientific papers and has received many awards and honors for his work, including Honorary President of the Czech Astronomical Society. A true Aries/Rat who claimed his truths through self-study.

Tuan Vo-Dinh (11 April 1948): A Vietnamese chemist, biomedical engineer and inventor. He specialized in the field of photonics, using laser and fiber optics to scan a patient's body rather than to operate to find out what is amiss. Vo-Dinh has been ranked No. 43 on a list of the world's top 100 geniuses. He has a very interesting life story as a true Aries/Rat.

Al Gore (31 March 1960): an American politician and environmentalist who served as the 45th Vice President of the USA. After his term as vice president ended in 2001, he remained prominent as an author and environmental activist, and his work in climate change activism earned him the Nobel Peace Prize in 2007.

Pedro Delgado (15 April 1960): A Spanish former professional road bicycle racer. He won the 1988 Tour de France, as well as the Vuelta a España in 1985 and 1989. He was a good climber, with an aggressive style, making cycling a spectacle sport and gaining him many fans. He works now as a sports commentator for TV Española during important cycling events. His opinions are respected world-wide.

Rafael Benitez (16 April 1960): A Spanish former football player and professional football coach. He is now the manager of Premier League club Newcastle United. He is the only manager in history to have won the UEFA Europa League, UEFA Super Cup, UEFA Champions League and the FIFA Club World Cup. He believes in very hard work to achieve success. In 2015 he became the controversial coach for Real Madrid football club, leaving soon after as his strong and basic tactics did not fit in with the egocentric group of elite players in the dressing room.

Neo Rauch (18 April 1960): An East German artist known for personal interpretations of his thoughts through his paintings. His realistic and surrealistic abstractions show his alienation towards the industrial socialist type of philosophy implanted in Communist East Germany, where material wealth overrides the spiritual development of the person.

Jennifer Garner (17 April 1972): an American actress. She gained recognition for her performance as CIA officer Sydney Bristow in the ABC spy-action thriller Alias, which aired from 2001 to 2006. For her work on the series she won a Golden Globe Award and a SAG Award. She works frequently as an activist for early childhood education and is a board member of Save the Children. She is also an advocate for anti-paparazzi campaigns among children of celebrities. An interesting life story as a true Aries

CHAPTER 2

ARIES/OX

THE ARIES/OX PERSONALITY

The combination of the sun sign of Aries having to merge with the Chinese Year of the Ox presents this child/youth with a challenge. For Aries is known to be a basic hunter type of individual, and the Ox is known for his slow and deliberate methods to achieve his targets; two very different mental and emotional traits that need to achieve a balanced compromise. So at times these birth signs can give this child the impression that he can become clumsy and slow, as an Ox. Yet on the other hand, when it comes to thinking as an Aries, he can be as quick as any other fire sign. So the contrast between these birth signs is significant. Happily his united survival instincts will see to it that the traits weld together through the heat of the Aries and the cool direction of the Ox. His parents will need to be firm in the guidance of their young child, but equally gentle as they accept their child's contrary behaviors, which at time will be aggressive and at others shy and reserved.

However, given time, this stoic personality will overcome any obstacle in his way, because he will be able to slow down his quick thinking Aries abilities, so that they no longer bother him. There is a saying, 'that through his deeds this Aries/Ox will shine.' And I can safely state this is a true statement. For this child has the ability to be charming when he feels there is a need, though when he is busy in his own world, he would just stubbornly get on with whatever task he is doing, leaving his social niceties for when he has the time to be pleasant.

The Aries/Ox's main personal ability is to focus on the job on hand, a renowned gift which in the end will pave his success. Neither is he is too worried about having just a few close friends, because he prefers to be a loner anyway. And throughout his life, the few friends who he will have chosen will be sufficient to keep him company, and to help him with his social life. In short, this Aries/Ox is an individual with the power and ability for cool planning, who will achieve what he wants; one way or another. For as an Aries he is very active in reaching his goals, and as an Ox his determination is second to none. In fact, in developing a well-balanced combination between these disparate birth signs, it will help this child/youth reach whatever peak he chooses to climb.

As an Aries he will pioneer his path, no matter the hardships. But he will have the benefits of his Ox strength of purpose, which is a huge advantage to help him succeed. So in a nut shell, though this union of disparate traits will not be an easy one to fuse, this child will be able to reconcile his different abilities by sheer hard work. Yet, once he is able to get over his first few hurdles, he will sail across any stormy sea simply because he is very well equipped to surmount any number of self-made problems. Principally as he is a basic hunter, with a very practical approach to achieve his goals, aided by a cool and calculating Ox, who hates failures.

THE POSITIVE TRAITS OF THE OX:

The Ox's positive traits are exactly right to settle those of the active and adventurous Aries, because the Ox is slow in his thinking and acting. He wants to be very accurate as he hates making silly mistakes. This diligent attitude leads him to behave with a solid and stoic manner, which is full of his strength of purpose. This single-minded focus is also full of industrious intentions, which is backed by his clear integrity, in order to be correct in most of his decisions. Happily this type of behavior breeds a self-control which amounts to being emotionally stable. And finally, as a happy surprise, this Ox personality can be very eloquent when he is expressing his thoughts and ideas. In resume, these Ox traits are strong and basic, but heavy to live with because making a rash judgment is not the norm for this year sign.

I also have to state that the Ox is known for his direct ways as he sets out to reach his ends. Though I have to admit that most of these positive traits will take some time to become obvious, for this child will spend much of his baby period scanning his environment and assessing his parents' behaviors, as he will want to make sure he is feeling safe before he spreads his wings. Being sure of himself is part of his security blanket. With this I mean, he expects the full support of his parents when he needs it. Because in the way he behaves at home and at school he wants to show he is responsible enough to earn the respect and support of his parents. Until he can look after himself, this self-belief gives him the serenity to help him to be in control of himself and his close environment. For this coolness is very much part of his main safeguard as a personality. One can say that the fusion of these positive traits should make for a great and steady personality, who is as durable as stainless steel, subtle like a rapier, and difficult to corrupt as gold.

THE NEGATIVE TRAITS OF THE OX:

The Ox for his part adds his weaknesses of being standoffish, more because he is shy rather than he wants to be awkward. But he can become stubborn at times, because he will not be pushed to act quickly. Then he will become biased towards the people he thinks belittle him, because he knows he is slow and at times clumsy. And to prove that he will not be pushed he will become a plodder, because making mistakes will make him feel vulnerable. Therefore this merger of distinct birth signs does add up to producing a child whose personality is constantly suffering internal conflicts when trying to sort out his priority as to what to do next. For, as an Aries, he is mostly full of action who wants to do things quickly. But as an Ox he will want to be more reserved, even slower, because he is more of a practical thinker than the Aries. So he will want to wait to see his chances of success before he commits himself. And added to this reserve is the Ox's strength of purpose, which in most cases will control the speed of the Aries. So that he will make sure the energy used to achieve any project is used for a good purpose. However, taken as a long term project, this merger is a good one for both these signs. Although it will take some time before this child's thinking patterns make the initial compromise to weld his different attitudes to life together.

I also feel I have to relate the story of why the Ox can at times become very resentful when he feels he has been cheated from his rightful place at the top. The story goes that the Ox came second to the Rat in the survival race that was organized by the ruling Chinese God who wanted to discover which animal was the most reliable to overcome and survive great difficulties. The idea was to find a cunning and intrepid animal, whose inborn characteristics mirrored the most basic of the known twelve human types of personalities which form the Chinese Twelve Year Personality Cycle. And it was the Rat who cheated the good natured Ox in the last stage of the race. This fact might explain why the Ox is now very suspicious of clever people who pretend to help, but are only looking after their own interests. But more of this later.

THE EARLY BEHAVIORS OF THE ARIES/OX:

Once the merger of the Aries/Ox traits begin to work together, particularly on the part of the Aries' negative traits, these will be modified by the Ox's stability. This will calm or control any rushed or aggressive decision from the Aries to avoid getting into personal problems. Because as this child's personality grows he will become a pleasant, though very active, young persona. For he will learn to handle and control his more passionate traits. Happily, because of his hard working and solid Ox's half, he will be able to use his abundant Aries energy to produce sensible behaviors, both at home and at school. In fact, at times to produce work which will be better than expected from either birth signs. Which makes me state, that in the majority of cases this mixed combination of different characteristics can produce very positive results. For what can turn out to be seen as the fiery temper of the Aries when he is frustrated, can be converted for positive use by the firm control from the Ox's strength of purpose. This stoic self-control can produce a calmer and more positive set of behaviors from this young Aries/Ox persona, unknown with many other Aries combinations.

This child will behave well enough as long as he is not too stressed. By this I mean this child, or even as a youth, should not be pressed to do too many tasks simultaneously. For this pressure would cause his Ox half to reach overload at the imposed demands. On the other hand, his Aries half would want to rush to finish his jobs quickly, or choose the easy ones first, or even to leave the rest for others to do. For as a sly Aries he would say in his defense that he had become tired because he had to do all the work by himself. Sadly, these are the times when being born an Aries/Ox can bring tension into this youth's behavior. As part Ox he will want to complete his duties in his own time, but mostly without protest. But as an Aries he would not mind exaggerating a little to excuse himself from doing all he was been asked to do. So to avoid this impasse, which can unbalance this Aries/Ox's emotional stability, it is best to ration his chores by giving him one job at a time and expect it to be done with care and precision.

THE ARIES/OX AS THE FIRST BORN:

If this Aries/Ox is born the eldest in his family he would take charge of his siblings and except the same control over them as he is subjected to by his parents. He would always try to be fair, straight-forward, with a no nonsense style of commanding which would make him popular with his brothers and sisters. They would soon discover their boundaries as instinctively they would know his style of keeping order would keep them safe, at least when they are young. They would feel they could trust him, because he would always be there when they needed him. This would be the case if his parents have been disciplined with him in the first place. If not, he would then do what he thinks is right, becoming a little despotic or even aggressive if his siblings do not do what he tells them. His saving grace would be that he would support them in any fight they got into.

THE ARIES/OX AS THE SECOND CHILD:

If this Aries/Ox is born in the middle or is the youngest in the family, he would prefer to be left alone, to do his own thing. In his quiet way he might well think he knows better than his siblings in what to do and how to do it. Because of his self-image he will not want to appear second to anyone, so he would prefer to be alone, though there could be times when his solo behavior could cause some conflicts with his brothers or sisters. So to avoid problems he would at times join them in their games, though he would prefer to lead rather than just be a hanger-on with nothing to contribute. But if at any time this Aries/Ox child becomes annoyed because he feels he is being bullied or misunderstood, he would not stop until he got his own back. For he would see his siblings as his tormentors, so his natural revenge trait would switch on. And no doubt there could well be a confrontation to satisfy his need to get even. This trait has to be recognized by his parents and amended as soon as it becomes evident.

THE BEHAVIORS OF THE ARIES/OX AT SCHOOL:

At school this Aries/Ox child would most probably mind his own business and prefer to be reserved, while making sure he does what he enjoys, without getting into trouble. He would also focus on the work he is doing and ignore the rest of the other pupils if they are not doing what they should. But neither will he want to be seen as a softy, preferring to be seen as a strong independent learner who wants to get on. When further motivated by praise from his parents or teachers, he would produce work better than the average to prove his worth. For this Aries/Ox's aim will be to show that by working hard he can overcome his slowness to end up with better results than his quicker peers. However, being the best in class will not be his ultimate aim, for it would mean he would have to put extra stress on himself to keep up with the demands of being the best. And he is far too wise to get into that type of rat race.

At senior school there will be times when he would need the support of his parents and the understanding of his teachers, who would have to wait for him to complete his work. For his Ox part will demand he has to do his work properly, no matter how long it takes. Because to make a careless mistake due to him being rushed would not please him at all. For how else would he be able to consider himself as being superior to the rest of his class? Happily his Aries half will go along with this attitude, because being seen as superior would mean he can achieve a better image and gain more Kudos as a positive student. But to compensate his fond parents and teachers for their wait, they would be rewarded by knowing they have a hardworking and loyal solid student, who would be forever grateful for their patience and tolerance plus their constant support.

SOME PARTICULAR BEHAVIORS OF THE ARIES/OX:

There is a singular characteristic in this Aries/Ox's makeup which is different to most youths; if he ever gets into trouble at home or school, shouting at him would only stir him into anger and resentment. So the best method to deal with him as a growing teenager is to have controlled negotiations with him, not easy for parents or teachers when they are angry, but in this case it will work wonders. For tenderness is the best weapon to use in dealing with this Aries/Ox youth, who is potentially a hard worker and a future successful adult. There could also be times when this youth will show a naivety which would surprise any casual observer, but if this shy weakness is taken advantage of, then beware of the imminent consequences. For this wounded young person, who has a huge ego, is no fool when he gets wise to any abuse and he will certainly try to get even. So give this young Aries/Ox time to mature, but do not belittle him in any way by abusing his good nature.

As mentioned above, some traits of the Aries will be at logger heads with those of the Ox at times. Because of their very different speeds of learning, particularly when starting and completing any task. So what has to be understood by everyone dealing with this Aries/Ox's upbringing, is that he has enough conflicts within his own makeup to not need further contradictions or conflicts, from or with any other person or persons. Even if they are trying to teach him. So the answer is to go easy in demanding from him immediate good results, either at home or at school. These will come in due time, for this youth is a conscious worker.

SUGGESTIONS TO HELP THE EMOTIONAL DEVELOPMENT OF THE ARIES/OX YOUTH:

The Aries/Ox has great debating skills! So put these skills to good use by suggesting he joins some sort of drama or debating group. By practicing these skills he will be able to learn how to communicate his feelings, without feeling embarrassed. This ability will help him to overcome his hesitant fear of making mistakes and express why he is slow at getting his work done. A slowness which is caused mainly by his self-doubt, which annoys him as much as it does those around him. But by meeting other young people to debate with this interaction will surely motivate and truly encourage him to take on the extra classes, or even speech lessons. For these activities would certainly help him develop socially, to be able to mix with all and sundry without any fear of being misunderstood. For on average this type of youth would normally tend to become an introverted personality. However, one must not forget he is also half Aries, with an inborn need to show off! So these parental-enforced extra social activities should excite that part of him to stand up and express himself for who he is. For once this Aries/Ox has overcome his initial shyness he will feel less vulnerable to being ridiculed.

SUMMARY OF THE ARIES/OX CHARACTERISTICS AND BEHAVIOR:

☺ Versatile, adaptive, hardworking, reliable, patient, courageous, eloquent.

☹ Selfish, arrogant, stubborn, resentful, clandestine, solemn, undisciplined.

IF THIS CHILD IS MISBEHAVING:

He can become too lively and undisciplined, and stubborn when he is disappointed with what is happening around him. His passion to have his own way can be annoying. When frustrated he can be arrogant and selfish, believing that he knows best. To overcome this crisis he's then impulsive to achieve his wishes immediately. When angry, he will seek revenge in a clandestine way which will become obvious to his parents/ teachers.

This child hates being told off. Always speak to this child at eye level (in a non-threatening way) and listen to him before blaming him for being naughty. Being firm with him doesn't worry him at all, only it has to be fair in his eyes. When rebuking this child do not use threats or physical punishment. The use of emotional blackmail will provide excellent results. Making him believe that he can do better just by listening carefully and working slower, without fear of failure. Let him know that if he does fail, as long as he has tried his best he will be supported. Being strict with this child will help him find his boundaries. And when he is being stubborn, just ignore him and pretend he is not there.

FAMOUS ARIES/OX PERSONALITIES

Hans Christian Anderson (2 April 1805): A Danish author, prolific playwright and poet. He is best remembered for his fairy tales with 'The Little Mermaid' and 'The Ugly Duckling' being two of his most famous. The latter story was a description of his own life story, because he was quite an ugly looking person, and clumsy in his movements, as well as coming from a very poor background. But his inborn positive traits made him overcome all impediments and to become famous.

Vincent van Gogh (30 March 1855): A Dutch post-impressionist painter. His life was full of drama because of his controversial character. He was unsuccessful during his lifetime and was considered a madman and a failure. He became famous after his suicide and exists in the public imagination as the quintessential misunderstood genius. Now he is revered as one of the greatest and influential artists of the 20th century. Sad for him, being born an Aries/Ox personality made it very hard for him to merge his disparate characteristics, resulting in difficult relationships among his friends and family.

Sir Charlie Chaplin (16 April 1889): An English comedian who worked in Hollywood. He is considered to be one of the funniest comedians in silent films. He had an interesting life story, both as an actor and behind the camera. He received a knighthood for his positive influence in promoting the new-born film industry, though his own life-story was not that easy to piece together.

Sir Raymond Firth (25 March 1901): A New Zealand born ethnologist, best known for his research on the primitive Maori people. He was considered to be one of the most eminent social anthropologists of the last century. He was a long serving Professor of Anthropology at London School of Economics. He died at the ripe old age of 100. A typical Aries/Ox personality.

Paul Erdos (26 March 1913): A Hungarian mathematician. He was a prolific solver of mathematical problems and regarded as one of the greatest mathematicians of the 20th century. Though he was accepted as having a brilliant brain, he was also regarded as the 'oddball amongst other oddballs,' because of his eccentric life style. True to the average Aries/Ox personality.

Pierre Boulez (26 March 1925): A French composer, conductor and pianist of contemporary classical music. He was considered avant-garde in his methods of creating and playing his music. He wrote his music not to conform to that of the establishment, but as he wanted to play it. A true singular Aries/Ox persona.

Colin Powell (5 April 1937): An American 4-star General, who was the Chief Commander during the Persian Gulf War. When he retired he become the USA Secretary of State, the first and only African American to hold this prestigious position. All due to his being a true Aries/Ox hardworking personality.

Fredinand Piech (17 April 1937): An Austrian magnet, engineer and business executive who was the chairman of the Super Visionary Board of the Volkswagen Group. Whilst this German car and truck manufacture, which exports world-wide and has made huge profits, it has not always been in an honest way as the German car giant admitted cheating C02 emissions tests.

Elijah Harper (30 March 1949): A Native Canadian Indian and Chief of his Red Sucker Lake Community. He was the first Aboriginal member of the Legislative Assembly of Manitoba. Rarely can one person change the course of history for an entire country. Elijah Harper did. He was instrumental in blocking changes to reforming Canada's Constitution which, if passed, would do nothing to protect First Nations cultures or languages. An Aries/Ox defender of his tribe.

Horst Ludwig Stormer (6 April 1949): A German-born American physicist who was one of the co-recipients of the 1998 Nobel Prize in Physics for his contribution to the discovery of a new form of quantum fluid with fractionally charged excitations. He is emeritus professor of physics at Columbia University in New York.

Susan Boyle (1 April 1961): A Scottish singer who came to international attention when she appeared and won the TV program Britain's Got Talent. She was famously under-estimated by the audience and judges until she began singing. Her life story is a true reflection of the Aries/Ox personality.

Eddie Murphy (3 April 1961): An American comedian, actor, writer, singer and director. A top box office star, he is paid the 4th highest salary as a professional actor in the USA. He has grossed over $3.8 billion in the USA and $6.6 billion world-wide. A smart Aries/Ox entertainer.

Larry Page (26 March 1973): An American business magnet and computer scientist, and co-founder of Google alongside Sergey Brin. In 2011 he became CEO of Google and is reputed to be worth $32 billion. A good example for many other Aries/Oxen to follow.

Brian Behlendorf (30 March 1973): An American technologist, executive, computer programmer and leading figure in the open-source software movement. He was a primary developer of the Apache web server, the most popular web server software on the Internet.

CHAPTER 3

ARIES/TIGER

THE ARIES/TIGER PERSONALITY

The combination of these two birth signs makes for a child who can become a charmer, with multiple talents which help him display his full potential. For he is very lucky to be born during these dates, as these signs are totally compatible. This means that this child has no inherent internal difficulties in matching and merging both of his inborn character traits. And I can testify that this is not common.

In short, this merger of the Aries with the Tiger provides this child with all the traits to magnify his desires, efforts and abilities so that he can do, or attempt to do, almost anything in any circumstance. This is of course if this lively Aries/Tiger child has been lucky enough to have received a strong and balanced upbringing, with the corresponding imposed self-control habits directed by his patient, but firm, parents. By this I mean this youth's personal social growth has been guided to combine and develop all his positive traits, while containing his weaker ones. For this is the only type of nurturing which will make sure this Aries/Tiger child will be able to make the best use of his natural born potential.

Though I do have to admit his parents will have had to use all their strength of character to control, and at times, to stop this sparky Aries/ Tiger from becoming too adventurous, as he sets out to self-test his many abilities. Because this Aries/Tiger will tend to burn up so much of his abundant energies that he can become a bundle of nerves, which will lead him into poor behaviors. A tired Aries/Tiger will find it difficult to obey the simple rules of family social behaviors. He can become anti-social in his demands as he tries to express his wishes, and at times in a very aggressive and selfish tone. Because once he is tired, this Aries/Tiger is unable to understand why he cannot get what he wants, when he wants it. Sadly this type of behavior converts him into a primitive single-minded hunter who can see no further than his wishes. Not the usual lively and pleasant child.

But the good news is that, in time his parents will find their best way to handle this awkward situation. Plus, once this Aries/Tiger has rested he will not feel so frustrated at being unable to continue with his hectic lifestyle. Though for him he would love to be on an unending carrousel of activities, because only through his self-discovery will he be able to understand what makes him tick. Though, if he was allowed to be active most of the time he would just collapse in exhaustion. My aim with these opening statements is to warn the brave parents and the teachers of the down side of this Aries/Tiger child, who can be fun to be with when he is in a good mood, but difficult when he is not.

THE POSITIVE TRAITS OF THE TIGER:

The Tiger personality is well known for the positive trait of his abundant energy, be it in short spurts, for he needs to rest between his dashing about, to recover after burning-up his explosive power. He will also demonstrate his high level of bravery to achieve his ends when he is after 'things.' Then, after he has achieved his goals and he is satisfied with himself, he will become most hearty and friendly. And to balance his daring risk taking and adventurous escapades, he is blessed with being born with a lucky star. And he does need it. But when the opportunity arises and he is not hunting as to what to do next, he will show he has the dignity and the authority to command. For he has some sort of 'magnetism' to attract followers, and this aura is made even better because of his natural benevolence.

In resume, most of these Tiger traits are not very solid or practical, as they represent an attitude as if his lifestyle is more like a 'flash in a pan,' only coming into being when he needs spontaneous action. This Tiger child is a powerful personality from the very moment he is born. But in this case, all this energy can and does help to put even more fire into his forward planning Aries half. So this union is a positive one, though it could become almost too much for this child to handle. Because he will have to learn to be self-disciplined to be able to control all his energies as it floods through his mind and body. However I believe the wise Chinese Astrologer choose wisely to equate this human character with that of the wild Tiger in the jungle, who hunts and lives alone, and who can be difficult to live with because of his very individualistic behaviors.

THE NEGATIVE TRAITS OF THE TIGER:

The Tiger, as we have come to know, has outstanding weaknesses. That of being impetuous being his main one, so he can be accused of being a risk taking, hot-headed individual. This attitude can lead him to become a boastful character, to cover up for his self-knowing weaknesses, plus to gain prestige and so hide from his failures. But he will boast only if he has to, such as when things do not work out as he has planned. Then he is quick to escape the awkward scene, to avoid getting caught out and punished. This habit leads him to become disobedient, as his intent is in getting what he wants and not thinking of the consequences. But when he does get into trouble for being selfish he will grudgingly accept his punishment. Because he believes that most of the things he does, or attempts to do, are okay in his estimation. Though he can get into dangerous situations as he tries to solve his self-testing adventures. These risk taking activities do not seem to bother him, or the problems he can cause the rest of his family.

But I have to state this Tiger child will not mean to be naughty, as he is just inquisitive. No wonder he is born lucky, for others might not survive his antics. Though he is not as foolhardy as it might appear, for he will take calculated risks and get away with it because of his sharp mind and steel-like nerves. In resume, this merger of the Aries and the Tiger makes for a child who could become better organized in his excessive behaviors, because of his basic logical thinking patterns. And in his actions he would also show a more controlled set of behaviors as becomes a cautious hunter. Though as an Aries/Tiger personality he will be always ready to help and charm his way out of most problems, because he has no fear in making amends. I also have to add that to his credit he is not malicious in any of his actions. Unthinking and selfish, yes. Though he will be ready to share his toys and his money with his friends, without demanding anything further back from them.

THE EARLY BEHAVIORS OF THE ARIES/TIGER CHILD:

Now after reading the above one may well feel that I have a soft spot for Tigers. And you would be right, as I am surrounded by them in my family. I have three; my ex-wife, a daughter and a son, so I became acclimatized or cauterized by their actions. For somehow or other they always find a way to escape when in trouble. As their charms and helpfulness go a long way to mitigate their misdeeds. I believe the best way to describe this Aries/Tiger is by stating he can be disarming in a 'devilish way', and at the same time a challenge to one's sanity! But at the back of this honest description is the fact this child is not as wild as I have made him out to be, for his Aries half is serious in his attempts to do the right thing for himself and his family, both while he is at home and at school.

This Aries/Tiger child will keep his parents very busy as they watch over this active fireball. He will tend to dash about doing as many things as enter his imagination, just to keep himself amused. Though he is not destructive in his activities, he just wants to know what is happening around him. At school too, he would be the same. But at no time will he aim to become a trouble maker. In fact when he is told off after he has been stopped from his wild actions he would look surprised; for in his mind he will judge whatever he's doing to be normal activity for a child.

THE ARIES/TIGER AS THE FIRST BORN:

Now if this Aries/Tiger is born the eldest in his family he would naturally take the lead almost without being asked, for being a leader would be his quest in life. For as an Aries/Tiger he has the natural authority and panache to lead, though sometimes his well-planned adventures have to be watched closely as he could over step the normal safety boundaries. He might go beyond what can be termed as a safe pastime, for it to turn and develop it into what can be foreseen as a down-right dangerous one. So to avoid any major disaster, while this brave Aries/Tiger is leading he needs to be told to keep within firm parameters. Even before he is allowed to take off with his brood. I can only state from experience that this child is no ordinary active child, for in his need to self-test his abilities, he will look to seek adventures when he sees the right opportunity. Even though these actions can get him into all sorts of tight corners, which he can get out of where others couldn't, simply because they do not have his gift for escaping. But by and large this restless young person can be depended on to do the right thing if he has been taught the need to self-control his actions for his own good.

THE ARIES/TIGER AS THE SECOND CHILD:

If this Aries/Tiger is born in the middle or the youngest in the family, he would try very hard to control his environment. If not, then this potential leader would be off to find his own amusement. For he would prefer to be on his own than be an extra in any group. One positive trait in his part is that at no time would he set out to be difficult as a matter of habit. Plus he would always want to help out (in his way of course,) wherever he finds himself. This is what makes this child so popular. With people he respects he would be generally proactive and helpful, naïve and trusting. His most important need would be to be allowed to develop his potential to the full, if not he might feel he is wasting his time. Something which he would certainly dislike and cause him grief. For instinctively he would know he has more than his fair share of good natural abilities, plus a bucket full of luck, which would urge him to do something with his life.

THE ABILITY AND NEED FOR THIS ARIES/TIGER YOUTH TO TAKE ORDERS:

But for all his active thinking and doing, this Aries/Tiger child is fortunate in that he can take orders from people he admires, so it is easy for him to follow his parents' instructions and later on, his teachers. The one weakness in this positive combination is his propensity to boredom. For this child is so full of energy that he must be involved in some sort of activity most of the time. Though he will need times to rest after he has spent himself. This means this child does not need to be on the go all the time, but it does help during the time he is resting that he is given some activity which he enjoys, like drawing, reading, playing with his Lego, or just helping round the house. Though his taking part in these activities might not last very long. So the best remedy is to vary his activities, to have a long list at hand of things he can do, and then leave him to decide how he spends his time.

I found this tactic to be the best way forwards to get this active Aries/ Tiger to do any set job. For example, with my Tiger son, first we both agreed on what he wanted to do and his ability to get it done. Then I kept my distance, trusting him to do his best and only helping him when he asked for my advice. The reward for him keeping his attention on what he was doing was a promise; that if he did complete his task properly he would be allowed to go off on his bike and ride round the go-kart tract near our home. But if he failed to complete his task as agreed, he would be stopped from leaving the house, or any other limitation which would show him my displeasure. I found that talking to him at eye level as I explained to him what was in my mind was a system that worked very well. In this way he would accept he had not fulfilled his part of the agreement and would agree to do better next time. Never adopt an aggressive or superior stance by standing over him, as he would find this challenging, as well as provoke him to stand-up for himself.

RECOMMENDATIONS ON HOW TO NURTURE THE ARIES/TIGER CHILD/YOUTH:

In general the best method to tame this Aries/Tiger individual is to show him lots of affection and firm guidance, and not to belittle him in front of his friends, even when he might deserve it. But, at the same time, make sure he is responsible for all his actions, and non-actions wherever he finds himself. This mode of behavior in treating him would see to it he becomes a good family member and at school, a good student. For the aim behind this treatment has to be to respect his individuality and his potential leadership, but at the same time to make sure he understands that he has to be responsible for his actions if he want to become a leader. Certainly he can be guided to become a delightful child by encouraging him to develop all his positive traits, like his courageous and unselfish actions, his affability in being unselfish, and his keen enterprise which will all lead him towards his self-improvement.

Though all the time this young Aries/Tiger will still need constant disciplining, which has to be firm and fair. For this strategy will serve as a stimulation to strengthen his loyalty towards his family and friends. Reinforcing this responsibility he needs to have towards his family and friends will help him to rein in his wilder activities. For I believe that a little emotional blackmail can be used to make this loyal Aries/Tiger become aware of his unsociable actions, which can rebound onto his family's reputation with negative results. And, being a basic thinker and naturally a loyal member with a duty to protect his tribe, this Aries/Tiger will think twice before embarking on any of his risky adventures which could rebound negatively onto his family's good name.

THE EASY WAY TO BLACKMAIL THIS SENSITIVE ARIES/TIGER'S BEHAVIOR:

So by using his family's good name as a form of self-control tactic, this fear will help this Aries/Tiger to check his naïve impetuosity. To avoid any trouble he will use his survival instincts, which are strong in this personality, as his defense system in calming himself down. Now, this strategy can seem a little farfetched when this Aries/Tiger is acting like a Jack-in-the-box, but believe me any firm but fair discipline coming from his parents and teachers will help to control this intrepid Aries/Tiger. For he will accept at his sub-conscious level that he needs these limits. As these restraints will give him an urge to self-motivate/self-improve, for he dislikes being told what to do as he tries to be his best, when he becomes conscious of what he is doing. For believe it or not, this Aries/Tiger youth is sensitive enough to want to give a positive image of himself, to overcome his wild or naughty reputation by being as pleasant as possible, without being subservient. His self-pride alone will make him conscious that he should try to do his best to prove he is not an up-start or a trouble maker.

THE GENERAL BEHAVIORS OF THE ARIES/TIGER AT SCHOOL AND BEYOND:

Thankfully, once this Aries/Tiger goes to school, he will discover very quickly that bright children can and do get more freedom for self-expression than the also ran. This discovery in itself is one way to tame his exuberance, for the trick is to make his studies feel easy for him so he is able to reach his goals without having too many difficulties. This tactic will mean advising him to take small steps in his learning. So he can see his success as reaching his targets, without too much trouble. This achievement in itself will further motivate him to improve even more, no matter how long the road is. For as long as he feels he is being successful he will try to improve. Notice I keep repeating he learns quicker, 'when he feels successful,' for he has a short fuse regarding the interest he has in what he is doing. For anything he feels is too difficult for him to do, he will automatically ask himself, 'Why am I doing this?' As he has so many other talents he will see no good reason to burn his energies on any matter which is going to cause him frustration.

The bait therefore to keep this Aries/Tiger paying attention on any subject he dislikes is to convince him that overcoming any academic difficulty will give him a good and positive feeling, which will be the basis for his future life. For this hard earned success will eventual allow him to become freer, from being told what to do, because he has self-improved to reach a high level of academic standards. This simple statement will impress his self-love, which will make him work harder on his weaker subjects, so he can plan and imagine his future as a successful personality.

There could be other times however when, in his eagerness to do as much as possible as quick as possible, he could become stressed which could provoke a break in his physical stamina. Because, though it might appear unreal, this Aries/Tiger's physical condition and nervous systems are not as robust as he would like them to be. In his restless daily actions he could burn out quicker than expected unless he takes his periodical rests. He should be firmly told this fact so that he avoids any overwork and damages his health.

Nevertheless, this Aries/Tiger can become a good academic student, backed by a very able sporting condition. Particularly as an individual athlete, as depending on others to support him to win is not his idea of partaking in sport. Yes, he will like to compete, but mostly as a single participant in any challenge.

SUMMARY OF THE ARIES/TIGER CHARACTERISTICS AND BEHAVIOR:

☺ Sympathetic, active, self-confident, loyal, popular, hardworking, charming.

☹ Rebellious, quick-tempered, stubborn, resentful, vain, blaming, impulsive.

IF THIS CHILD IS MISBEHAVING:

The Aries/Tiger child can become a rebel if he thinks he is being bullied, though he tries to be as helpful as he can. But only for short spaces of time, as his mind wonders looking for new experiences. This child can be quick tempered, at times cruel, and when he is tired he can be most annoying. He can be disobedient without thinking of the consequences of his actions and will blame others if he is found being naughty. He can speak out when he has been emotionally hurt, and his honesty can be embarrassing, as he will speak his truths without thought of the problem he may cause. If found being naughty, he can become enraged, angry at everyone, including himself. For this self-confident child there is no greater humiliation than failure.

It is best to deal with this child with firmness through understanding and love in that order. Before chastising him ask him why he acted as he did. And always be at eye level when you're speaking to him, for any intimidation will only make him wilder. This child is intelligent enough to understand logical reasoning, so making him sit down to listen is a good method to calm him down, or sit him by himself to allow him to think about his misdeeds. Tiger children are tough, yet very sensitive. As an example of their acting-out behaviour, he can set up a dramatic scene by crying, even throwing himself onto the ground. In this case, quietly pick him up and sit him down, or if older, just walk away and pretend to leave him. His fear of being abandoned will make him react. My tiger son would sometimes use these tactics. When he was old enough, I would leave him to walk home on his own, but he had to wait till I came to go into the house, giving him time to think about what he had done.

FAMOUS ARIES/TIGER PERSONALITIES

Francisco Goya (30 March 1746): Considered the most important Spanish artist of the late 18th and early 19th centuries, and immensely successful in his lifetime. He is often referred to as both the last of the Old Masters and the first of the moderns. His style of painting was bold, colorful, and honest, and by using light as a focus he was able to highlight the drama in his paintings. Goya is a very clear exponent of the true Aries/Tiger creative personality.

William Wordsworth (7 April 1770): A major English poet, who with Samuel Coleridge founded the Romantic Movement in English literature with their publication of the Lyrical Ballads. This new-style spread to Europe and influenced many other poets, who followed their new and more open style for writing verse. He is a prototype for the Aries/Tiger personality; bold, clever and daring.

Herbert Henry Dow (26 March 1886): A Canadian born American chemical industrialist. He is known as the founder of the Dow Chemical Company in 1897. He started off by improving the output of a small factory in Ohio. Later he developed a method to improve production to a bigger scale. He was an inventive and a powerful personality; a true Aries/Tiger personality.

Isambard Kingdom Brunel (9 April 1806): An English mechanical and civil engineer who is considered one of the most ingenious and prolific figures in engineering history, an engineering giant and one of the greatest figures of the Industrial Revolution. He changed the face of the English landscape with his ground-breaking designs and ingenious constructions. Brunel built dockyards, the Great Western Railway, a series of steamships (including the first propeller-driven transatlantic steamship) and numerous important bridges and tunnels. His designs revolutionized public transport and modern engineering. An Iconic Aries/ Tiger personality.

Brooke Astor (30 March 1902): An American heiress. Her third husband left her an immense wealth, which she was told to share-out among the public institutes of America. By the time she died at 105 years she had given away over $195 million to charities and other organizations.

Octavio Paz (31 March 1914): A Mexican poet, diplomat and writer. For his body of work he was awarded the Spanish Miguel de Cervantes Prize in 1981. In 1982 he was awarded the Neustadl Prize in Literature. In 1990 he was awarded the Nobel Prize in Literature. A Smart Aries/Tiger.

Hugh Hefner (9 April 1926): An American entrepreneur, magazine publisher and playboy. Founder and owner of Play Boy magazine, he was well known for his lifestyle and enjoyed being seen among much younger women. He was an advocate of sexual liberation and freedom of expression as well as a political activist and philanthropist. He had the Tiger magic which attracts beautiful people.

James Hillman (12 April 1926): An American psychologist and lecturer. He founded a movement based on the study of the archetypal personality at the famous Jung Institute in Zurich University. He then became the head of the Institute. Later he retired to go into a private singular lifestyle. For he felt he had reached his limits, so he just retired, rather than be seen as an old rope. This is the true reaction of an older Aries/Tiger personality.

Marvin Gaye (1 April 1938): An African-American song writer, musician and record producer. He helped shape the sound of Motown in the 1960s with a string of hits, earning him the titles 'Prince of Motown' and 'Prince of Soul'. He has been posthumously bestowed with many awards and honors including the Grammy Lifetime Achievement Award, the Rhythm and Blues Music Hall of Fame, the Songwriters Hall of Fame and the Rock and Roll Hall of Fame. A true direct Aries/Tiger personality, ready to create a new trend because of his vitality.

Kofi Annan (8 April 1938): A Ghanaian diplomat, who served as the Secretary General of the United Nations from 1997 to 2006. He was the recipient of the Nobel Peace Prize in 2001. He was charming, but with strong personal views. A good prototype for the Aries/Tiger personality who knows what he wants.

Jacques Herzog (19 April 1950): A Swiss architect and co-founder of the world famous design studios, Herzog & de Meuron, known for their architectural style and inventive use of both natural and artificial materials. Noteworthy and prominent projects include the Tate Modern in London and a dramatic steel latticework structure known as the Bird's Nest that was the main arena for the 2008 Olympic Games in Beijing. Both he and his partner have been highly decorated for their work.

Carlos Sainz (17 April 1962): Spanish Formula One racing driver. He was the winner of the World Championships for Toyota in 1990 and 1992. He loves to drive in the Dakar desert race, as it presents him with all the adventures he wishes to have. Yet he makes sure that he has all the necessary rescue equipment with him before he starts his race. Very typical Aries/Tiger behavior. In fact in 2018 he finally won the Dakar race in South America.

Victoria Beckham (17 April 1974): An English businesswoman, fashion designer, model and singer. She rose to fame in the late 1990s with the all-female pop group Spice Girls, and was dubbed Posh Spice. She is wife of David Beckham, the world renowned footballer. She has since become an internationally recognized style icon and fashion designer. In 2011 her design label was named designer brand of the year in the UK. A positive version of the female Aries/Tiger, who never stops improving her image.

Sergio Ramos (30 March 1986): A Spanish professional football player, he is captain of Real Madrid and the Spanish national team. He is the winner of many trophies and World Championships. He is known both for his skills and his temper. He seemed to collect Yellow and Red cards by attacking cheeky players because he does not like to be messed about.

CHAPTER 4

ARIES/CAT

THE ARIES/CAT PERSONALITY

The combination of the Aries and Cat birth signs helps this child generate a peaceful environment, with refinement and wisdom around him/herself. But at times there is a need for this child/youth to have an adventure, or a daring experience, during inexplicable situations. This intrepid behavior is all down to his Aries half, which needs some sort of action to satisfy his need for self-discovery. Because this daring action can be seen as a self-testing challenge to discover his limitations. Then after passing his self-test this Aries/Cat will feel pleased with himself, for overcoming his challenges is very much part of his self-esteem building to buttress his security blanket. Which for him means his parents will fully back him in all his endeavors because he tries to be as obedient as possible. Though he will try their patience on more than one occasion with his impromptu adventure seeking.

Sadly this need for self-challenging is a constant conflict within this child's mental makeup. Because he has to face the question of, 'to be or not to be,' as it becomes an inherent dilemma in this child's character. For the courageous power of the Aries, having to mix with the timid but intelligent calmness of the Cat, makes this fusion of traits an uneasy mixture to weld. Even though both of these signs are basic hunters, the way they go about their hunting differ in strategies. Naturally, as soon as possible their separate survival instincts will force a mental agreement between his two halves, so their different hunting techniques will settle down to reach a compromise. After which this child/youth will enjoy the peace and the sanity of the Cat, rather than the constant self-testing needs of the passionate Aries.

However, this challenge to fuse these very different thinking attitudes has to be faced, endured and shared. Firstly within this child's internal thinking patterns, then among his family members, and then also with some of his teachers, who will find it a challenge to understand this child's contradictory forms of behaviors. Happily this mental struggle will diminish in time, for this Aries/Cat's self-love instincts will see to it that this complicated fusion is accomplished as quickly as possible. Aries is the most basic of aggressive hunters, while the Cat is the most sophisticated of trappers, so their different techniques will have to merge by adapting both forms of hunting methods, which will make sure this child/youth does his best looking after himself and his interests in every possible way.

THE POSITIVE TRAITS OF THE CAT:

The Cat's positive traits are that of being tactful; always being diplomatic and sensible in the methods he uses to achieve his ends. This is helped by his smooth fineness, which leads him to appear virtuous. And to show a superior attitude when he is among those people who he wants to impress, he will study those around him and gather as much personal information from them to store in his armory. He will use this knowledge later when he feels it will be an advantage for him to show understanding. But at the same time, he will use this private information to add a touch of leverage when he wants something from the person he is with. For his aim is directed to his self-improvement; to become socially cultured, very well informed and to develop an aura of class. Now to make sure all these controlled traits add up to him being seen as prudent, reliable and pleasant, he will act with supreme caution. But nevertheless, for all his calmness the Cat is a very ambitious personality. And neither will he stop at doing anything underhand to overcome any obstacle on his path. This last trait gives the Cat a strong back bone, which I shall enlarge on later.

I also feel I have to add here I have a big respect for the Cat, because this animal was chosen by the Wise Chinese Astrologers to depict a particular personality. We all think of the Cat as a tame, and domesticated animal. But we tend to forget it is also a hunting animal as well. So though this Cat personality might be seen as gentle and nice, shy and vulnerable, I can state this is a cover up. He has inborn abilities which help him to survive; seeming to always land on all fours and get away from many self-made dangers almost 'scot free.' And to add to his many survival skills, his ambition to reach or achieve his goals are undisputable very feline. I can also add that this Cat is certainly not weak, even though he does not like fighting or getting hurt while he is hunting. This last trait can be the reason why this Cat is often called a Rabbit. But I see this character as a hunting animal, who will not hesitate to attack if he has to protect himself or his family.

THE NEGATIVE TRAITS OF THE CAT:

The Cat's weaknesses are his squeamishness at the sight of blood or pain, as these sad scenes can become a major drama for this child. And to cover up this fact he becomes secretive as he tries to hide his feelings of vulnerability. Then he will hesitate before taking any action until he is sure to achieve what he wants. To the point that he will wait until he is completely safe and sure that he will succeed. For in this Cat's self-esteem he has to be correct in whatever he does, and if he finds he has made a mistake he will happily lie to cover up his blunder. Though sadly at times he will wait so long to make up his mind that he loses the opportunity to achieve his goals. This will really annoy this patient child, and after which he will be ready to blame others for his failure.

This anger then causes him personal discomfort and inner frustrations, which lead him to develop self-made complexities. In short, these upsets will further make him become even more fearful, before making a stand about his work or his beliefs, which will make him appear spineless. However his saving grace, and to get out of any embarrassment, is that he can act almost any role without hesitation as he is mostly full of pretense, and by so doing he can present himself as a calm and peaceful yet strong personality.

The good thing about the merger of these birth signs is the basic intelligent and sensitive positive traits from both signs will, with the love and appropriate home nurturing, cancel out the more negative ones. As this child's self-esteem can guide him to the right level of social behaviors, because neither of his birth signs is weak. So to balance these inborn disparate traits both signs will have to work hard to make sure their inborn diverse traits do not cause him any problems. Though happily, when most of his diverse traits do merge, they will produce a strong and creative individual. To the point he will be able to act with the aplomb of a hardened ambitious fighter, using his single-minded strategy to climb up any social ladder which suits him at the time.

THE EARLY BEHAVIORS OF THE ARIES/CAT CHILD/YOUTH:

I can happily state that when both of the different inborn traits do merge the result is a positive one. Though there will always be an inner conflict within this Aries/Cat's thinking patterns. As he will be continuously sorting out his priorities on how best to achieve his ends without causing too much of an upset. For at times he will appear to be timid, slow and reserved, and at others he will want to have his own way, fast and furious. However, the good thing is because this Aries/Cat is quick to learn, he will soon discover that his urges for action will mostly get him into unnecessary confrontation with his parents. So, to lead a quieter life, he will try very hard to control his Aries urge to self-indulge by working hard on his self-discipline. So by using his cunningness rather than his fire, he will still achieve what he wants.

And if he is lucky to be born into a balanced happy family system, this Aries/Cat will see the advantages for him to learn to self-control, for this will avoid upsetting his beloved parents. As when this intrepid Aries/Cat child does calm down, he will be praised and rewarded handsomely! Because all those who live with him will know just how much effort he has had to make to conquer his Aries quick-action impulses, as he searches to discover his limits through his self-testing adventures. However as this tamed child is still part Aries, he will still need to have these action-packed moments, during which he will on occasion behave in ways which are not entirely acceptable. But this Aries/Cat can forgive himself, as he is only searching to have a daring adventure to test his survival skills. So parents, please be gentle with him after he has been up to some naïve devilment, because he is following a deep seated need to explore his potential.

NURTURING THE ARIES/CAT CHILD/YOUTH:

This child will be seen as a mixture of bravery and timidity. But at the same time his parents will notice there is a certain cunningness about their young offspring which can match any adult's. For this child needs to discover and he will use all his intelligence to seek the evidence and assurance that he is being loved by all this family. This evidence will make him feel he has a protective security blanket. By this I mean, that as a pleasant Aries/Cat youth he has the full support of his parents when he needs it, because he tries to behave properly at home and at school.

This need to seek protection from his elders will be his basic intention before he leaves home to go to school and beyond. For when this astute Aries/Cat is feeling safe, there is very little he will not try to do, or even takes risks, which other Cats would shy away from. Of course he would be a good student and do his best at times when he has not to prove how brave and daring he can be. I have to keep stating this dichotomy inborn in his mixed behaviors, for this Aries/Cat can either be an open risk taker, or a sly obedient charmer with a hidden agenda, to get what he wants, with the least possible risks or effort.

THE ARIES/CAT AS THE FIRST BORN:

Now if this Aries/Cat child is born the eldest in his family, he would conform to all the rules and regulations put on to him by his parents. However, these norms will have to be introduce to him in a friendly way, without threats or forceful pressure. For any aggression shown towards him will be answered with his own aggression, for he is not part Aries for nothing. Though his timid behaviors as the leader of his siblings will demonstrate his interior conflicts. For one moment he would be direct, forceful and ready to take any action, then if challenged on whether he is going to take the lead he would retreat, as if he does not want to have anything to do with any previously planned activities. In time his siblings will soon get to know about his hesitations, so they will either take advantage of it, or guard against it. For at times their bigger brother will dominate them fiercely.

Yet by the time this Aries/Cat persona is eleven to thirteen years, he would want to learn how best to behave within his family unit, so to avoid causing any trouble with his leadership strategy. For his main wish is to fit in within his family's home policies, for this behavior would guarantee his own self-protection. However at the same time, he would demand to have a big say as to what his family is planning to do. For he is well aware that he has a complex personality, so to avoid creating any upset he would like to be involved with most of his family's plans. As his involvement will help him to become more familiar with his parents, so he can get to know what is expected from him, and they will better understand his type of thinking patterns; from calm to hectic and avant-garde.

Because there could be times when he might cause an upset with his siblings by saying he wants to do one thing to please them, and then another to please his parents. And even worse, to do something quite unexpected from his first intentions. This complexity of behaviors should be accepted, even helped to develop, so this confused Aries/Cat can see his need to self-control his impulses, when he is acting like a daring Aries. So rather than be blamed or ridiculed because of his changing attitudes, he should be helped to understand that changing his mind so quickly does upset those who are depending on him. Particularly after he has produced a plan of action, which his siblings are involved in. But to mitigate this youth's uneven leadership role it has to be said, that deep down all he wants to do is to please everyone around him, become popular and to be loved for who he is.

THE ARIES/CAT AS THE SECOND CHILD:

Yet if this Aries/Cat is born in the middle or the youngest in his family, he would play his double game which would be natural in his behavior. So his brothers and sisters would just have to get used to his strange ways. For at times he would become boisterous and even challenge them to become their leader, while at others he would become shy and retiring, even refusing to take part in their daring activities. However he would try his best not to confound his brothers and sisters with his alternating behaviors by diverting their attention to what he can do for them. For as an inborn actor he can become very funny, as well as to be willing to help out when needed, without demanding anything in return.

SOME ODD BEHAVIORS OF THE ARIES/CAT YOUTH:

There can be times when in his Aries 'showing off' mood where this Aries/Cat youth could be seen as an upstart or a pretender in the way he wants to show his superiority. In truth, enough to upset those who had seen him as a timid personality and had made fun of him. Because after this show of power and even belligerence, his tormentors will wonder how best to treat him in the future. As behind this Aries/Cat's pleasant exterior, there is a personality who will be delighted to get even with anyone who tries to belittle him. Which could well happen when these bullies least expect him to act.

Neither will they have to wait too long before this Aries/Cat delivers his stored anger towards them, because they had hurt his feelings. For this secretive youth can wait to get even with his tormentors until he knows there will be no major come back because of his revenge. For his streak of Aries anger can turn this peaceful child into an avenger. And he will get his own back by either belittling all those who made him feel intimidated, by literally attacking them physically, or by proving that they are 'as thick as bricks' in public.

THE ARIES/CAT AS AN INDEPENDENT PERSON:

This ability to use his Aries half to fight his corner can make this Aries/Cat youth into a potential leader at spasmodic intervals, which if encouraged could help him become more self-confident. This statement can sound farfetched, as at other times this youth will prefer to hide from the limelight. But in his general development, this Aries/Cat youth should be encouraged to step up into the action. For this attitude would avoid him being so hesitant when he is about to do something which might involve taking some risks. Because supporting his Aries half should be the aim of his parents and teachers, so to get this Aries/Cat youth to take on the risks of making mistakes. As this bravery in turn will show he has enough common sense to lead, and this fact will improve his self-esteem. For I believe there is a huge hidden talent in this youth for him to be able to produce some classical artistic work, which will show his in depth knowledge of the traditional cultures he so much loves!

Yet as part of his day to day acting, this Aries/Cat youth will pretend he is an easy going personality, who is prepared to go with the flow just so as not to cause any trouble. But when it comes to eating, he is a fussy eater and will not mind being difficult. Because if he does not like the look of his meal, he will not eat it, even though he will go hungry. Also foods which have a sharp taste will also be seen as too much to swallow. In time his taste buds will mature at least to try strange foods, but while this fragile Aries/Cat is still a youngster, eating in general and what type of food he eats, will be a challenge for all concerned.

Sadly this struggle with his eating habits could develop into tension at meal times. And to allow this to happen is not a good idea. So the best solution would be; to come to some agreement with him as to what type of foods he will eat, plus the promise to try different meals or go without! Then when he reaches an age when he can be allowed to provide his own meals, like doing his own shopping and cooking, he should be given this challenge. I believe this time consuming task might get him to eat whatever he is being given by his mother!

SOME INTERESTING FACTS ABOUT THE ARIES/CAT'S EMOTIONAL DEVELOPMENT:

There is one other interest which fascinates this curious Aries/Cat's personality, which is his love to discover important historical events which have had important influences in the way the world has developed. So as soon as this interest is evident, he should be encouraged to do his own research. For the one way this youth can show he is different is through his academic work. This and the fact that some Aries/Cat youths are natural detectives can turn him into an investigator. Plus this study can help him understand more about himself, for he is well aware he is not like most children. For example he might enjoy learning to play a musical instrument, rather than being out there with the other kids. For he will not mind practicing for hours. But his reward would come when he shows off in front of his family and friends.

But though this Aries/Cat will enjoy his academic studies, it is also very important he should be motivated to take up some sort of individual sporting activity. Certainly to improve his self-defense tactics. For though he can be ready to defend himself, he might not have the necessary power, stamina or even the strength, nor the body weight to provide him with the needed capacity to avoid getting beaten up. So the suggestion is he should take up some sort of martial arts training or maybe weight lifting to build up his body, and so be able to withstand any physical confrontation. This training will indirectly lead him to gain weight and strength, and certainly help him to eat a wider range of foods to calm his appetite.

SUMMARY OF THE ARIES/CAT CHARACTERISTICS AND BEHAVIOR:

☺ Intelligent, thoughtful, friendly, understanding, courageous, self-confident, adventurous.

☹ Over cautious, selfish, blaming, cunning, stubborn, adamant, grandiose.

IF THIS CHILD IS MISBEHAVING:

This child is ambitious, artistic, talented and very sensitive. As a child he is easy to nurture with the proviso that he receives the best of treatments and given most of what he wants. This child is full of energy, aimed at great things and great accomplishments. He has very few doubts and doesn't scare easily. He is not afraid to take risks and doesn't avoid difficulties. However, he fears failure and at times he can be over cautious, missing out on golden opportunities. Then he will blame others for his failure, or even lie to hide his anger. If he feels deceived and insulted, he will find a way to achieve justice.

Rather than console him, ask him why he acted as he did. For it is up to him what he has to do, rather than to blame others. His aim is to always be successful. If he gets over defensive, even acting unloved as a form of emotional blackmail, just pretend that it is his fault he feels that way. The best way to deal with this child is to be firm with him when needed. Yet very understanding when he is uncertain on what to do. The point is he has to solve his own self-made problems. Being aware of his mixed inborn Aries/Cat traits should guide parents/teachers to use their instincts, rather than their temper, to lead their child onwards into his creative progressive future.

FAMOUS ARIES/CAT PERSONALITIES

Max Erns (2 April 1891): A German painter, sculptor, graphic artist and poet. A prolific artist who was the pioneer in creating the 'Dada Movement,' which others followed. He was the first to paint what he saw in his subconscious, by going into the realms of the unknown areas in his mind.

Rudolf Serkin (28 March 1903): A Bohemian-born pianist. He is widely regarded as one of the greatest pianists to interpret Beethoven's music as the composer wrote it, and wanted it played. In 1939 he moved to the USA and became naturalized citizen, and in 1963 was awarded the Presidential Medal of Freedom. He toured all over the world and was revered as a musician's musician, a father figure to a legion of younger players, and a pianist of enormous musical integrity.

Joe Foss (17 April 1915): An American ace fighter pilot during World War II. In 1943 he was awarded the Medal of Honor for his bravery, which he earned during the Guadalcanal Campaign. A true American patriot, who fought the Japanese in the Pacific theater, showing his Aries daring abilities, but with the Cat's caution.

Martin Fleischmann (29 March 1927): A British chemist noted for his work in electrochemistry. He and Stanley Pons designed a machine which they claimed could do 'cold fusion'. It did not work, but they continued to experiment to discover how to improve their invention. His life story truly reveals the characteristics of the complex Aries/Cat personality.

Cesar Chavez (31 March 1927): An American farm worker who became a civil rights activist. He with Dolores Huerta co-founded the National Farm Workers Association to improve working conditions. These workers mostly came from Mexico, as low cost immigrants, but Cesar managed to raise their rates of pay and their living conditions.

Sir David Frost (7 April 1939): An English journalist, writer, media personality, comedian and television host. He was famous for his style of interviewing, making his guests sweat. For his contribution to the news media industry he received an OBE in 1970 and was knighted in 1993. He was clever and direct, yet smooth and daring. Very much the Aries/Cat mixed personality.

Seamus Heavey (13 April 1939): An Irish poet, playwright, translator and lecturer, first at Belfast University, then at Harvard University in the USA, and lastly in Oxford University, England. He was awarded the Nobel Prize in Literature in 1995 for his work in humanities. He is every bit an Aries/Cat personality.

Dusty Springfield (16 April 1939): A British pop singer and recording producer. Her career extended from the 1950s to the 1990s. As an artist she was among the best in the world. She was awarded an OBE by Queen Elizabeth II and was inducted into both the Rock and Roll and UK Music Halls of Fame.

Dean Kamen (5 April 1951): An American entrepreneur and inventor. He dropped out of college to follow his desire to invent, and use his innovative ideas to create things. He has now more than 150 patents to his name. He designed and produced the Segway PT, an electric self-balancing personal transporter.

Tommy Hilfiger (24 April 1951): An American fashion entrepreneur, founder of his own brand as a designer of fashionable apparel for men, women and children. His range of clothes is wide, from the sporty to the formal. A true example of a smooth Aries/Cat personality who loves style and money!

Mark Jacobs (9 April 1963): An American fashion designer for his Marc Jacobs fashion brand with over 200 stores in over 80 countries. He has had a huge influence in modern clothing with his designs demonstrating a fine balance between style and usefulness. He is ambitious and hardworking. In short a true Aries/Cat who uses all his inborn talents to make BIG money.

Doris Leuthard (10 April 1963): A Swiss politician and lawyer. In 2006 she became a member of the Swiss Federal Council. From then to 2010 she became the Head of the Department of Finance, becoming the highest ranking official in the Swiss Government. A position favored by most Aries/Cat personalities.

Garry Kasparov (13 April 1963): A Russian/American chess Grandmaster and former World Chess Champion. He is also a writer and political activist. He is considered to be one of the greatest chess players this century. He was ranked number one for 225 out of 228 months, winning 15 consecutive tournaments and 11 chess Oscars.

Maria Sharapova (19 April 1987): A Russian tennis player, now living in USA, she has won 27 WTA tournaments and 4 Grand Slams. She has been awarded various trophies as a top athlete. She is known for her unyielding fighting spirit and the will to win during her 12 years on court.

CHAPTER 5

ARIES/DRAGON

THE ARIES/DRAGON PERSONALITY

The combination of these two very powerful birth signs gives this child a huge responsibility as part of his/her destiny. For he should develop most, if not all, of his positive traits as they are almost unique to this child. So as a payback for the privilege of having been born during these important times, the parents of this Aries/Dragon should provide him with all the necessary facilities to urge their offspring to self-improve. For not many people are graced with so many positive traits, which should provide this child/youth with the potential to further his self-development, which other people can either admire or even envy. Because most people would see this child's general character and behaviors to be attributed as a gift from the Gods.

So to give credence to this reputation, this child can become a positive, loving and charming youth, but in his case it would be completely natural, without being taught or influenced. Though he would have to be in a good mood, to stand out as a top star. Certainly this image would not be true, when he is not achieving what he wants, and he is angry. But then at the same time he would have the sheer determination of an adult when it comes to getting what he wants. For he is able to use tactics as sophisticated as any adult, unknown among other youths. For I believe in the term, 'by hook or by crook,' must have been coined for him. Because with his charms most adults should find it difficult to negate his wishes. As he can be so persuasive, by using his type of magical proactive talents. Simply because as an Aries/Dragon he is so engaging, funny and attentive, that his act would appeal to everyone's vanity. However, the development of all these positive behaviors will depend on how this child is natured at home. Ideally, (and I am wishing) in a balanced home life with the right proportions of love, firmness and parental guidance.

It is therefore a pity I have to describe this child's negative traits later on, because this child could become a little 'monster,' when he is using all his magical powers to become a selfish and intolerant personality. But this is the way we form our personal character, as we are all born with our Ying and Yung energies, or our negative and positive inborn traits. And this child has them both in huge amounts. So his parents better be prepared to have a challenging time while they have this Aries/Dragon at home, as he matures from baby to young person.

THE POSITIVE TRAITS OF THE DRAGON:

The unique Dragon enjoys the positive trait of his strength of character, for he is always looking for fame, which is always pushing him to become successful in most of his endeavors. This is backed by his enthusiasm and aided by his blind bravery. Happily, because he is gifted with good health, he can do more than can be expected. These traits naturally lead him to become a good leader, who has an understanding of his followers as individuals, so that he can get the best out of them. He is also a soft and emotional sentimentalist, who dislikes seeing the people he loves suffer, because he cannot control their fate. These traits can be judged to be mainly action led, mostly to avoid losing face. Though he has his good looks to overcome his many naïve mistakes.

I have to state here that the Dragon is the only 'fictitious' animal in the Chinese Twelve Personality Signs, as the wise Chinese astrologers could not match this person's magical characteristics with any known animal specious, so they had to go into their mythology to discover an animal which can spit flames! And can act in extraordinary ways, to later repent for his flame throwing!

THE NEGATIVE TRAITS OF THE DRAGON:

The Dragon's weakness is his rigid type of thinking, as this type of safe and slow thinking patterns delay and even slow down his actions. But he does this, to prevent himself from making silly mistakes. So he keeps to what he knows. But this hesitation leads him to mistrust himself because he doubts his own potential. We can all suffer from this feeling as it helps us from overreaching ourselves, but he covers up his doubt by boasting about his many triumphs, which then leads him to feel unsure and dissatisfied with himself. Because he expects more from himself, even though he knows he has limited experiences. Most of the time this Dragon instinctively knows he doesn't have the skills necessary to fulfill most of his promises, although he will think that his brave, blind enthusiasm will make up for his weaknesses. However in resume, this merger between the Aries and the Dragon can become a very pleasant and magnificent union. Because it can offer physical and mental strengths and solid common sense, backed with basic survival instincts.

HOW TO NURTURE THIS ARIES/DRAGON CHILD/YOUTH:

Happily the positive traits from both birth signs will down play most of the negative ones. However, when this Aries/Dragon is challenged because his Aries half has been a little too quick at showing his aggressive moods, then his Dragon's half will lose his temper, show his sharp teeth and shoot out his flames in ferocity. So beware of offending this character by pointing out his weaknesses. Yet as usual I have to add, that the best way for this youth to become a well-balanced personality is for him to be brought up in a loving, yet firm and well directed home, where there is a strong and fair discipline. And that the general academic education he receives is given in a strict and personal way. Then I can predict there is every chance that this Aries/Dragon will do very well for himself.

THE EARLY BEHAVIORS OF THE ARIES/DRAGON CHILD/YOUTH:

Therefore, the good news is that when all these different traits from both birth signs merge, they produce a child who has so much potential, both in his positive and some of his negative characteristics, that there is every chance of him evolving into a charming and caring personality. Though he will need much controlling for his own good, and that of his family! For certainly he will need to receive a formal upbringing, as any haphazard treatment in his nurturing will only lead him to take over and try to rule the household himself. Because without having to obey strict guidelines, from both his parents, and his teachers, this young lad will want to do his own thing, regardless of the consequences. Plus, in order for him to carry out his duties as a family member or a student, he will need the necessary self-discipline to put all his inborn talents into practice. For there is no other way this eager Aries/Dragon will be able to self-improve. Without first being taught to exercise his self-discipline, which in the end will give him the prestige he likes to have to back his self-esteem.

I state this because as this Aries/Dragon child/youth matures, and he begins to show his range of positive talents, it would naturally lead to him becoming the center of any activity at home or at school. And to cap it all, he could become a good student, though his parents and teachers would have to be firm as they guide him through his studies to get him onto the right path to fulfill his potential, and to avoid his ego getting in the way. Because with so many creative talents at hand, this child must be guided to put them all into their correct action. As this learned self-control should help him develop all his inborn gifts to the full. For this Aries/Dragon youth has to be made to realize that by using and developing all his inborn abilities, he will be fulfilling his inborn duty and personal responsibilities. Now with this statement I also involve his parents, who have to provide all they can to make sure their offspring does achieve the successes he is able to reach. This means they have to show their interest, and at times their unselfish efforts, to make sure this Aries/Dragon is brought up within their traditional values.

A WARNING AGAINST THE CHARMS OF THE ARIES/DRAGON:

The one draw-back with all this close attention by his parents is, that at home this Aries/Dragon child could easily become spoilt; his charms and mature thinking can make him a star within his family circle. My fatherly mature warning is, do not fall into this trap. Because he is liable to abuse his privileges and then 'rest on his oars.' For he can easily become a spoilt brat in his demands, to have his own ways without making any effort on his own part. Sadly I feel I have to make this blunt statement even though it does sound negative.

THE ARIES/DRAGON YOUTH AS THE FIRST BORN:

If this Aries/Dragon is born the eldest in his family, he would rule the roost without any problem. In fact, he can be so impressive with his many exciting ideas, that the others would follow him and serve him with their loyalty. Though he could become a little lazy at times, for he would expect his siblings do his work. Then if they don't, he could get upset as he would feel neglected. For, as with everything in nature, each privilege has its own balance, and all gifts come with their corresponding down side. For on his negative days, this Aries/Dragon could become naturally arrogant, then lose his temper when he is frustrated and act like an impish so and so. Therefore, to help him avoid showing his more selfish side and to avoid having these unpleasant situations, his parents need to spend some time in having one to one talks and negotiations with him. For if they have to point out that he can become nasty, he would lose his impeccable plus charming reputation, which naturally he would not like at all.

This type of threat that he would lose his bright reputation would be the best leverage to use with this young Aries/Dragon youth. Particularly when he neglects to do his duties, as being single-minded he prefers to do his own thing, so he will forget to do what he has been told. But under the threat of losing his reputation this would make him think twice about neglecting his chores and not showing his nastier, selfish side. This wake-up call would make him realize he has to do what he has been told, if he is going to enjoy his privileges. Experience says most arrogant people can be tamed through the use of subtle negotiations, blackmail really, but it is a good way to teach this reluctant Aries/Dragon to do his duties.

Therefore from my experience his parents, and later on his teachers, have to become very firm with this talented youth so he does fulfil his duties and so improve himself as a pleasant helpful personality. Because no doubt he will have been told he is a multi-gifted persona, so he better work hard to develop all his talents if he is going to reach his proposed targets. And as he is the first born in the family, his image has to be 'whiter than white.' Another subtle way to use the same emotional manipulation he uses himself with the rest of his family.

THE ARIES/DRAGON AS THE SECOND CHILD:

If this Aries/Dragon is born in the middle or the youngest in his family, his sheer independence and charms would win over his older brothers and sisters, so he could end up as their leader. But only sometimes. It is common knowledge that at times to impress this Aries/Dragon keen personality can promise more than he can deliver. When this does happen he will have no hesitation in blaming the others, for not coming up to his speed. So his defense will be to become the victim and feel upset and let down, almost becoming negative and resentful.

During these occasions his parents have to explain to their Aries/Dragon child that he has to learn to gauge the delicate balance between what he can do, and what he wishes to do. So when he fails he has to accept, that for the time being while he is still young and inexperienced, he will be limited in what he can fulfil or accomplish, no matter how hard he tries to fulfil his promises. Though I believe he can be told, that there is nothing wrong in making promises, which later he might not be able to fulfill, as long as he has tried to do so by doing his best.

THE ARIES/DRAGON'S EMOTIONAL DEVELOPMENT:

Once this Aries/Dragon youth has learned his limits of what he can do and cannot do, he will be able to reach the position of not letting others down or avoid feeling bad about himself. I am going on about this feeling of being let down, but this emotion will be felt by this sensitive Aries/Dragon child as a negative self-doubt because, for all his panache, he has an inferiority complex, as the balance to his upfront panache. So this aspect of not wanting to 'lose face' is vital for any Dragon, and when the naivety of the Aries is added, this youth will feel tormented when he cannot accomplish all he has promised. This I believe is the down side of wanting to be popular and at times arrogant, because of his outward need to show his prowess which can be sorely dented.

THE BEHAVIOR OF A TEENAGE ARIES/DRAGON:

I have to admit that having a budding Aries/Dagon leader in the household will not be an easy matter to live with. For there will be times when his Aries/Dragon's naivety and impulsiveness, can take them by surprise. As he might well do something really silly to impress his peers or friends, without thinking of the consequences of his actions. Hopefully with luck, this Aries/Dragon might never get into any major troubles, but if or when he does he should be reprimanded and warned firmly. Because any further misdemeanors will rebound on his standing and reputation. So if his aim is to remain popular he better learn to self-control his extravert behaviors. I believe after a good telling off, his self-esteem alone will deter him from getting into further adventures. But possibly not for long, as his need to show off is very much part and parcel of his makeup, or at least his Aries half. Nevertheless, his parents should keep on him to be aware of not getting into any adventure which could develop into a dangerous past-time. Particularly when he wants to demonstrate his abilities as a dare devil leader.

NOTES ON THE ARIES/DRAGON'S SCHOOL WORK:

I have not mentioned what this Aries/Dagon can get up to at school, because he could turn out to be a real star, or a pain. I say this because if his teachers are fooled by his superficial attitude, that he will try to do his best while in fact he is only showing off, he will not advance very far. However if they firmly and demand his best work, there is every chance he will do just that. Because as a charming Aries/Dragon he needs to be pushed gently but firmly towards his academic goals. However where this Aries/Dragon youth might not need urging will be on the playing fields. There he should do rather well if he is made the leader or the organizer of his group, with the promise of earning Kudos for his efforts. As his ability to encourage others to do their best is his great strength, and at times his weakness. For he will fall for the same flattery he gives out when he receives this praise himself. But there again, if he does get on with his work to develop most, if not all his positive talents, I see nothing wrong in pumping-up his vanity trait. For we all have this weakness, though some of us fall deeper than others. In resume, I believe this double birth sign the Aries/Dragon is almost magical, but it needs polishing to bring out its luster.

THE ARIES/DRAGON EMOTIONAL DEVELOPMENT:

One trait which is common with most Dragons is his propensity to falling in love, with any person he/she admires. This might be a fleeting self-made romance, but the consequences can have all sorts of dramatic results, from becoming a love sick stoker, to a passionate helper of the chosen personality. And it will depend on how the other person reacts as to how long this infatuation will last. But one thing is for sure, it will upset the rhythm of this Aries/Dragon's behavior while this emotional situation lasts. Because he can become an absent minded youth, to a risk taking Romeo, as he will want to impress his sweetheart. So his parents have to be warned of the drama when all this romance falls apart and this sad, lost Aries/Dragon feels broken hearted. Thanks heaven being a lively Aries/Dragon he will get over this make belief romance quicker than most. For he will soon fall again to make up for his last fiasco. Now the best way to get this romantic Aries/Dragon onto the normal teenage self-love path again, is to get him to try to concentrate on his studies. Because as he nears his end of school examinations he should try very hard to achieve positive results. Which will set him up for life. At least this is the best way to sell his future to him, with the motto of 'the more I learn the more I can earn.'

SUMMARY OF THE ARIES/DRAGON CHARACTERISTICS AND BEHAVIOR:

- ☺ Charming, cheerful, optimistic, smart, confident, responsible, hard-working, active.

- ☹ Dominating, aggressive, arrogant, strong-willed, intolerant, manipulative, prideful.

IF THIS CHILD IS MISBEHAVING:

This child is one on his own, different to most other children. He can be a charmer with all the attributes of a smart thinker, but will try to dominate wherever he goes. So he develops his own self-made authority which he covers with his charm. He prefers to do his own thing rather than to be told what to do. At times he bites off more than he can chew. He can be impulsive and intolerant of other people's shortcomings. It's better to be friends with him as he can become aggressive if thwarted and angry when he is corrected. Yet he is capable of creating many sensible ideas which he can get others to put into practice. He can arrogantly defend himself which can undermine his parents/teachers authority.

The best way to deal with this apparent strong-willed child is to get him to understand that, for all his impressive image, he has to back his ideas with hard work. He can be made to feel ashamed when he does not do as he is told. But use kind words to stop his defensive reaction after he has misbehaved. For angry words will only make him defend himself with vigour. An eye-to-eye logical talk will make him realize that he has been found out; that he's not as good as he portrays. As he certainly doesn't like to be criticised (particularly in front of his peers) playing up to his pride and his abilities will encourage him to perform better. At times it is good to just let him suffer before coming to his help, as taking things for granted can be one of his weaknesses. Support this child by playing on his ability to be charming rather than aggressive to get what he wants. At times meet his force with calmness and detachment. This will frighten him more than an open argument with him.

FAMOUS ARIES/DRAGON PERSONALITIES

Donald W. Douglas (6 April 1892): An American who loved flying. He became the chief designer for the Martin Aircraft Company. Then he was funded to design and build the Douglas Aircraft. The most useful aircraft of its day, which achieved great success during World War l I. He was the first to design and build an airplane with a 'pay load' greater than its own weight. A smart Aries/Dragon inventor.

Robert Watson Wall (13 April 1892): An English inventor who discovered that by bouncing radio waves into the sky he could detect flying objects. This helped him to invent the Radar, which helped the Allies to win World War II. This invention made it possible to detect on coming enemy aircraft long before they arrived and so prevent the enemy from dropping their bombs. Even to shoot them down while they were fully loaded.

Arshile Gorky (15 April 1904): An Armenian/American abstract expressionist painter of great influence. His work is seen as the result of the suffering and loss he experienced during the Armenian Genocide by the Russians. He pretended to be related to famous people so that his work was accepted, though his paintings were good enough to gain fame on their own merit. He was also a very good art teacher.

Christian Anfinsen (26 March 1916): An American biochemist. He shared the 1972 Nobel Prize in Chemistry with Stanford University for his research in the connection between the amino acid sequences in the brain cells. He was offered a University Fellowship at Harvard Medical School.

Gregory Peck (5 April 1916): An American actor famous for his epic blockbuster roles in top box office films. He was honored by President Lyndon Johnson with the Medal of Freedom in 1969 for his work as a Humanitarian for, as a good Aries/Dragon, he never forgot those in need.

James Lovell (25 March 1928): An American astronaut and Commander of Apollo 13, which developed a critical failure while in flight, but because of the crew and ground-control's 'iron nerves,' the mission was brought home safely. He became a national hero for his cool nerves under terrific pressure.

Maya Angelou (4 April 1928): An American award-winning author, poet and civil rights activist who is considered as one of the foremost African-American creative voices. She demonstrated all the qualities of the Aries/Dragon as a hard working personality.

Wangan Maathai (1 April 1940): A Kenyan political leader and founder of The Green Belt Movement in Africa. She was the winner of the Nobel Prize for Peace in 2004, and the first African woman to receive such a prize. She was also featured in a documentary about her work in 2008 which made her an icon to be followed by future generations.

Herbie Hancock (12 April 1940): An American pianist, composer and band leader. He was one of the first jazz musicians to embrace the music synthesizers and 'funk music.' He did this while playing with the Miles Davis's Quintet. As a good Aries/Dragon he was not afraid to show off and break new ground in music to improve his image.

Richard Allen Griffin (15 April 1952): An American federal judge on the US Court of Appeals for the Circuit appointed by George W. Bush. Previously he was a judge on the Michigan Court of Appeals. He comes from a family of lawyers of high standing, and is considered to be a deeply conservative jurist.

Elle Macpherson (29 March 1964): An Australian model, actress, business woman and TV host. She is well known for her record '5 cover appearances' in the Sport's Illustrated Swimsuit Issue. She is known as 'The Body', but she also has a very sharp brain and has made the most of her attributes as a self-confident Aries/Dragon persona.

Bjarne Riis (3 April 1964): A Danish professional cyclist known as 'The Eagle of Herning' He is famous for winning the Tour de France in 1996 and was hailed as Denmark's sports figure of the century. His life story depicts all the good traits of the Aries/Dragon personality.

Russell Crowe (7 April 1964): Born in New Zealand but works as an actor in Australia. He has been in many epic and historical films playing the tough, indestructible hero. He is also a musician and producer. He won an Academy Award as Best Actor in 2000 for the film The Gladiator.

Lisa Querrero (8 April 1964): An American award-winning journalist, actress, sportscaster, TV host, model and mother. She is known as 'the hardest working sports reporter,' as she goes where the action is, no matter where.

CHAPTER 6

ARIES/SNAKE

THE ARIES/SNAKE PERSONALITY

The combination of these two birth signs is not easy to fuse, as their inborn traits are quite disparate. This means there are individual characteristics inborn in these signs which will take time to merge. As they merge, there is a good chance they can produce a strong imbalance in the natural emotional development of this child. The reason for these emotional upsets is caused by the need for each sign to develop its own emotional thinking patterns, which are mostly different from each other, and simply because their sentiments and emotional intelligence spring from two different areas of the brain. The Aries is basic and passionate in his needs, while the Snake has controlled emotions; waiting to see which is the best way to act in order to achieve the most with the least effort on his part. The Aries can erupt quickly and spontaneously at the smallest spark in the air, with such force his energies can rock any steady vibration in his vicinity. While the Snake is always trying hard to make sense of all this wasted energy.

But the good thing about this merger is that all the inborn traits will meld together thanks to the calmness of the Snake. The fire of the Aries will be controlled from its excesses, and at the same time the Snake will become more adventurous as a creative risk taker, in truth more than can ever be imagined. The Aries is naïve and blunt and the Snake is cunning and smooth, but in mixing these traits they can produce a child who is versatile and brave enough to do what is usually unexpected of a cool Snake. And this welding of traits will take place because both signs have very acute survival instincts, which will ensure this child develops all the necessary skills to do very well for himself in this life. The basic ingredients to achieve success are present; when the Aries basic brave hunter traits are welded to those of the cool and creative Snake it can become very positive. As the union of the brawn and the brains can achieve more than expected from either birth sign. For the Snake is be able to perfect his ingenious actions, aided by the panache of the Aries who fears no one.

THE POSITIVE TRAITS OF THE SNAKE:

The Snake has keen intuition, which works more like a fact-finding computer and which gives this child a sense of knowing. In fact, one can say that his sensitivity is close to being psychic, and in moments of self-preservation it is. This ability leads this child to become full of discretion, knowing when to speak up and when to keep quiet, which is backed by his compassion to empathize with human emotional weaknesses. This sensitivity allows him to become very creative in most of his artistic skills and abilities. In total all these traits are coming from his emotional Intelligence, inherent in this sign, and like all emotional signs, Water signs mostly, they are subject to the cycle of the Moon and the highs and lows of the tides.

By now the reader will begin to understand the see-saw type of personality inborn in this child. And this is only in describing his positive traits! We in the West might think of the Snake as a repulsive animal, but in the East it is seen as a high-end personality, with charms and graces which are popular in China. I can only add that the Wise Chinese Astrologers knew what type of human behavior they were describing when they called this Year Sign the Snake. And finally, to round off this positive portrait of this wonder child, this Aries/Snake is mostly very attractive, not only as a personality, but also in physical looks too.

THE NEGATIVE TRAITS OF THE SNAKE:

The Snake's weaknesses are his love for elitism and his extravagance, which leads him to get stressed when he does too much to impress. But only when he is with those who he thinks will add to his superior image. This stress can then cause him to appear lazy, as he seeks a quiet rest to regain his lost energies. And to get his rest he will pretend that he is busy, when in fact he is not interested with what is going on around him. In truth, he would like to appear to be unique or exclusive, for he likes to do as he pleases, undeterred by what is expected of him. So to achieve this exclusive attitude he will act as if he is superior by being full of vain presumptions. For Snakes love to look 'cool.' And finally this cool child has the ability to tell lies, to uphold his make belief world. For once he has thought of a story which will back his actions, he will stick to it as if it is true, thereby becoming an expert in the art of plausible deception.

This does not mean that this personality is a born liar and is not to be believed, but that almost as a form of habit he can lie to get out of self-made problems. But for this Aries/Snake this habit is not a fault as the rest of us would judge, for he can turn this ability into an art form to get away from difficult situations, which he dislikes. Because in his creative mind, to avoid trouble with a side step is not a fault, but a quick escape from compromising circumstances. Finally I have to state that the fulfillment of this child's positive development depends entirely on the way he is being brought up, more than any other child. For this Aries / Snake needs to feel the love, care and attention from a pair of happy and balanced parents within an organized family structure.

The above prerequisite I know is not easy to create, particularly when both parents are working. But I state the above because I believe this lifestyle is the best to nurture this active and creative Aries born Snake youth. For living within a secure home background will help to weld together all his many positive traits, with the added advantage that this will help the wise Snake become more proactive, as he is fired up by the motivation and the energy of the Aries. Though at the same time, this child/youth has to cope with the weight of having to merge all his negative traits from both his birth signs. No wonder this child/youth has to become a manipulator, just to come to terms with himself, let alone co-habit with his family, and later within his community.

THE CHARACTERISTIC OF THE ARIES/SNAKE CHILD/YOUTH:

In my experience I have come to the conclusion a sensitive child is an intelligent one, and in the case of the Aries/Snake, it is really true. For I know of an Aries/Snake artist who loves to go to Morocco to paint. There she finds the heat, the daring adventure, the romance and the mysterious all rolled into one experience, which allows her to become very creative. Added to this is the feeling of a tinge of danger and adventure, which is compensated with the knowledge that the Euro goes a long way in Morocco! This description rather encapsulates the spirit of both her signs, for she is also an active, good looking, entrepreneur with her own riding school in Marbella, Spain.

But to return to this charming Aries/Snake personality who has emotions to burn, but his way. For he can become rather selfish in the way he goes about his lifestyle. Added to this single-minded attitude, he has a great advantage over the other Fire signs of Leo and Sagittarius, for he has a vast well of creativity, plus an enormous innovative bag of talents, which he can put into use most of the time. With this I mean, that by using the most simple of materials, he can fashion from bits of paper and some glue a beautiful flower or the shape of a new style car. This fountain of creativity leads him to have endless plans and projects, which are fashionable, easy to create and are pleasing to the eye. And added to these talents he has the charms and tenderness to melt anyone's heart, so that he can get away with not doing all the tasks he is supposed to do at home and later on at school. For he can be a clever little Snake at avoiding any household chores, believing them to be beneath his dignity.

THE ARIES/SNAKE AS THE FIRST BORN:

At home when young, this Aries/Snake will become the center of attraction, because he will do all that is necessary to be seen as the popular child in the family. For, as already mentioned, the Snake child is normally an attractive looking individual, and if one adds the jollity of the Aries, one can imagine the star-like born actor within the family. So if this Aries/Snake is born the eldest in his family he would contrive that his younger siblings do all the housework for him. And they would mostly do it without a murmur, for he can be very helpful with their school work and, if needs be, lie for them when they get into trouble. At the same time, this Aries/Snake would also keep them very busy with his type of creative work, as long as they cleaned up after themselves. And added to this creativity, he would console them when they get hurt, or are disappointed when they are frustrated in their wishes.

THE ARIES/SNAKE AS THE SECOND CHILD:

If this Aries/Snake is born in the middle or the youngest in the family, he would pretend he is far too little, or incompetent, to do any household chores, with his fertile mind thinking up excuses to fit every occasion. I now set out to explain how to find remedies to help his parents, and later his teachers, on how best to deal with this lazy Aries/Snake. I recommend the best way to avoid having daily confrontations with this sleek avoider is to negotiate with him, what else can he offer to do? In this way he can offer a solution to save face, and so give his parents and teachers a whip hand to keep him to his words. I believe this dislike he has towards cleaning up is due to his own self-image, plus his dislike in doing ordinary things, while he is only thinking of his self-fulfillment. For as an Aries/Snake he knows he is very creative, and doing menial jobs such as cleaning is wasting his time. Because he firmly believes, as the clever exclusive persona he is, that cleaning is not what he is meant to do with his time. Yet, when he is busy creating his own fertile dreams, he will spend hours working intensely, involved in his own world and not minding what mess he gets into.

THE ARIES/SNAKE AT SCHOOL AND HOME:

At school this Aries/Snake will readily offer to help others with their work, and so slyly miss out in cleaning the art room after a craft lesson. I do not want to make too much of this weakness, but it does annoy others when they catch onto his avoidance tactics. To avoid helping in the classroom he can become busy tiding his books or finishing some of his work, or even helping others with their studies, anything other than helping to clean up. But at no time will I accuse this brave Aries/Snake of being dirty. Untidy yes, but as regards his personal hygiene, this child will want to be clean and smart all times. Now at home he will also find ways and means to avoid helping, as he can give creative reasons as to why he cannot help, because he is busy watching a TV program for information, or he is reading an important book, or he is just finishing his homework, etc. It is almost a point of honor to avoid any task he does not enjoy. Yet, when he is interested in impressing his mother or special friends, he can become a human dynamo.

THE ARIES/SNAKE AS AN ACTOR:

Turning to another positive talent of this Aries/Snake's persona, and one which is a very important part of this young personality, and that is his acting skills, for he is a natural actor. And he is able to display this talent by the dramatic way he can demonstrate his ability to perform simple comedy. For as part of his self-protection system this Aries/Snake is very observant, so much so that he will be able to pick out the odd and funny mannerisms of those around him. Then he can cleverly exaggerate their idiosyncrasies, and so provide himself and others with some fun. I suggest this talent might well become a very positive element to develop at home and at school. When this Aries/Snake feels the circumstances in either place has become charged with emotional tension he will quite spontaneously think of some sort of comedy to lighten-up the environment, to release the stress by providing some form of comic relief. And he will do this almost automatically because, as a sensitive Aries/Snake child, to live in any stressful situation will upset him and do him no good at all. For he will capture the anger and resulting tension within himself, and this vibration will make him feel very uncomfortable.

THE ARIES/SNAKE'S LOVE FOR HIS PROPERTY:

On another level of behavior, this Aries/Snake has an odd habit in the way he reacts when he is trying to protect his property. For his parents might discover that their off-spring does not like to share his toys with his other siblings, fearing his toys might get damaged or even broken. For almost without wanting to show just how selfish he is, he will demand his toys are treated with the same care as he shows when he plays with them. When it comes to using his property, he can become quite firmly conservative in the way he expects his items to be used. However, the funny thing is when he uses other children's toys he does so without a thought of how he uses them, or whose they are. The reason for this disparate behavior can be found in his Snake's emotional attachment towards his own property, with little thought about the property of others. This attitude can be seen as openly selfish, but he does not see it this way, because he states that when he is allowed to play with the toys of others, he can do as pleases because they trust him.

Again I have to explain that the Aries sign is the first of our astrological signs, which is accepted as the most primitive of the signs, but when added to the sophistication of the Snake, this child can think himself able to do as he wishes. Why? Because when he compares his creative skills or his survival abilities with other children, he can see he can do most things better than them, even without putting himself out. To give an example, if he wants to show off and demonstrate how he can play the piano, fly a kite or sing a song, he will be able to show a higher level of skill, simply because he would have studied beforehand as part of his survival instincts, or else he would not show off. Naturally, not all Aries/

Snakes are that good with their manual skills or creative abilities, but a good average of them are.

HOW PARENTS/TEACHERS CAN DEAL WITH THIS ARIES/SNAKE CHILD:

But rather than dampen this Aries/Snake's self-belief that he is superior, parents and teachers should urge him to use this trait to get him to work harder to achieve more, because he can. This is not an easy matter for any growing young person who is faced with having to work harder when he feels there is no need to feel pressured, for he would prefer to coast along. Because being a Snake to work under pressure makes him he feels stressed, and he hates feeling stressed because it depletes his energies. But then as a keen Aries/Snake youth who wants to impress those people he wishes to use at a later date, he will try to conform to what is expected of him. When needed, he has the ability to become creative and dynamic, so getting fussed because he has to work harder is only part of his adrenaline rush, which he will only use when there is no other option.

THE ARIES/SNAKE AS A MATURE STUDENT:

One very important point to make here is the Aries/Snake's ability to learn his academic subjects quickly, as long as he is not stressed. Because, with his Aries quick mind and the creativity of the Snake, this youth can become like a sponge in his learning of a subject which he feels will help him in the future. So I suggest to his parents and teachers that they use the same tactics he uses to achieve his ends - emotional blackmail. Let him believe that by working hard at the subjects he needs, they for their part will help him achieve his targets. For his eventual aim is to reach 'the easy life' he is always day dreaming about. The catch is he has to pass most, or even all, of his school exams before his parents will support him to go to college or university. I can guarantee, because I have done it myself, this cunning Aries/Snake will work as hard as is needed to succeed.

SUMMARY OF THE ARIES/SNAKE CHARACTERISTICS AND BEHAVIOR:

☺ Wise, smart, polite, foresightedness, charming, purpose-orientated, hard-working.

☹ Impatient, manipulative, quick-tempered, impulsive, controlling, possessive, cautious.

IF THIS CHILD IS MISBEHAVING:

The Aries/Snake child is charming and cultured, and sensitive to the environment he lives in. He has the ability to anticipate events so he can manipulate situations to his own advantage. He is gifted at being very creative and emotionally cool, using his emotions to achieve what he wants without burning too much of his energies. His strength is his ability to be sympathetic with those who he loves, or wants to help in solving their emotional problems. The other side of him is that he may seem to be much wiser and emotionally stable than they are, often appearing to be older than their years, which makes for a very cunning and selfish personality. He can sometimes be deceitful in achieving what he wants, with little thought of others, creating his own version of the truth (which in his mind is real) to achieve what he wants. He can also become easily stressed by self-imposed pressures when he wants to impress those who will later help him. This makes him impatient with those who do not do what he wants to do. He can be heartless, inconsistent and possessive, seeking revenge with those who have upset him. This is not a child that forgives easily. He can also become jealous of those who can do better than him simple because they are able to work hard.

The merger of these birth signs produces a child who can be complex one moment but very clear and direct at others. This child can be negatively influenced in a confused environment. He needs strict guidance with tender love and understanding, but demanding from him his best, because he can. Being very firm with him will show that he might by cunning, but his parents are no fools. Indeed this will make him feel safer at home. Using logic rather than blame will help this child listen rather than defend himself. He can demonstrate mature thinking, but mostly to avoid doing what he has been told to do. He can experience quick changes in mood and may lose control of himself. Placing him in a calm, quiet atmosphere will allow him to sort out his emotions and reflect on what has happened. It is good to remember that this child is psychic and that he can use this ability to undermine any idea he is not in favour with, therefore guide this child to come up with a better idea. The goal has to be for him to think and act, rather than to criticise or give excuses.

FAMOUS ARIES/SNAKE PERSONALITIES

Wilhelm C. Röntgen (27 March 1845): A German mechanical engineer and physicist. He was the recipient of the first Nobel Prize for Physics in 1901 for his discovery of electromagnetic radiation in a wavelength range known as Röntgen rays, or X-rays as we have come to call them, and which heralded the age of modern physics and revolutionized diagnostic medicine.

Harvey Cushing (8 April 1869): An American neurosurgeon. He developed many of the operating procedures and techniques that are still basic to brain surgery today, and his work greatly reduced the high mortality rates that had formerly been associated with brain surgery. He became the leading expert in the diagnosis and treatment of intracranial tumors. He is often described as the father of modern neurosurgery. A truly outstanding personality, as one would expect from a clever Aries/Snake personality.

Gustav Vigeland (11 April 1869): A Norwegian sculptor. Admired for his creative imagination and his prolific production. He worked in bronze, granite and wrought-iron, making what some termed the weirdest statues in the World. But his creativity is seen as charming, very much like the Aries/Snake that he is.

Béla Bartok (25 March 1881): A Hungarian composer and pianist. Together with Franz Liszt, he is counted amongst the greatest composers from Hungary, and considered one of the most important composers of the 20th century. He was inducted into the Grammy Hall of Fame in recognition of his compositions.

Viktor Frankl (26 March 1905): An Austrian neurologist, who survived the Nazi concentration camps because of his knowledge of how his brain works. He used this knowledge to help him overcome stress. He is a famous author, having written a book on his dramatic prison experiences during his imprisonment. His motto was, 'I have to keep sane, because I have something to live for.'

Randy Brooks (28 March 1917): An American jazz trumpeter and bandleader. He started to play the trumpet at age 9 and by 11 he was touring with Rudy Vallee. He then worked for other bandleaders, until in 1944 he formed his own band. He was a very popular and successful creative bandleader, who was daring as an Aries, and then sophisticated as a Snake.

Mort Drucker (29 March 1929): An American caricaturist and comic artist best known as a contributor for over five decades on the widely famous Mad magazine. He specialized in satires on the leading feature films and television series, to amuse himself and his readers.

Vivienne Westwood (8 April 1941): An English fashion designer and businesswoman. She was largely responsible for bringing modern punk and new wave fashions into the mainstream. She came to public notice when she made clothes for Malcolm McLaren's boutique in the King's Road, London. It was their ability to synthesize clothing and music that shaped the 1970s UK punk scene, dominated by McLaren's band, the Sex Pistols.

Bobby Moore (12 April 1941): An English professional footballer. He captained West Ham United for more than ten years and was captain of the England team that won the 1966 World Cup, for which he was awarded an OBE. He is widely regarded as one of the greatest defenders of all time. He won a total of 108 caps for the England team, which at the time of his international retirement in 1973 was a national record. He was a great leader, using his intuition to get the best effort and performance from his players.

Sir Andrew Wiles (11 April 1953): A British mathematician and a Royal Society Research Professor at the University of Oxford, specializing in number theory. He has worked on a number of outstanding problems in number theory and is best known for proving Fermat's Last Theorem. He was knighted in 2000 for his contributions to mathematics and science. His life story depicts the different traits of the Aries/Snake personality.

Jose Maria Manzanares (14 April 1953): A Spanish bullfighter, the third generation of Matadors from the same family. Although he began studying Veterinary Science, he soon realized that his vocation was bullfighting and by 1971 he had become a fully qualified bullfighter. Described as "the maestro of the maestros" he became one of the largest figures in the sport. He was a classic matador with elegance, great technique and artistic quality. A good mix for the Aries/Snake personality.

Eelco van Asperen (11 April 1965): A Dutch computer scientist. He was an associate professor at the Erasmus University in Rotterdam, at the School of Economics. On the first web pages created he was credited as having contributed to the World Wide Web project. He ported to a PC the line-mode browser (the second web browser ever created.) The browser was the first demonstrated to be portable to several different operating systems.

Francisco Ribeiro (15 April 1965): A Portuguese cellist, composer, conductor, vocalist and record producer. He was the founding member of the group Madredeus, a group that combined traditional Portuguese music with influences from contemporary folk music. He was always active in creating musical projects, a pity he died at age 45 from liver cancer.

Mark Spencer (8 April 1977): An American computer engineer. He is the original author of the GTK+ based instant messaging client Gaim; the LZTP daemon 12tpd and the Cheops Network User Interface. He is also the creator of Asterisk, a Linux-based open-sourced software. He is the founder of Digium, an open-source telecommunications supplier, most notable for its development and sponsorship of Asterisk. He uses the daring of the Aries with the inventiveness of the Snake to create new ways of using the computer to work for him.

CHAPTER 7

ARIES/ HORSE

THE ARIES/HORSE PERSONALITY

The combination of these two birth signs of Aries and the Horse Year can produce a child who shows early promise, as he can demonstrate his true potential quicker than most other children. For with his charming smile and his proactive clear intentions, he is a natural winner. Because as a keen Aries/Horse child he will have this ability from the very moment he can learn to grin. For as he grows older he will readily develop his manual skills and his sociable dispositions, which will make him popular with his peers and with the adults who live with him. However, for him to develop as I have described above, he has to live in an action packed and happy family environment. Plus he will expect the same interesting activities later on at school. For when he gets bored there is the danger he might get into some mischief. Not intentionally, but because he wants to be involved in doing or making something to test himself and discover how far he can go in his free daring adventures.

Because, as an active Aries/Horse child he needs to be involved in some action, if this causes him some upset he will defend himself by blaming others for not being involved with his projects or his games. For how else will he be able to develop his many talents? And this need will make this intrepid Aries/Horse child/youth become a handful, as he shows his independence within the safety of his family's care. Or even at school, as he wants to learn through experiences and his self-testing by using his many practical skills. Naturally getting into trouble is not his intention, neither does he want to cause any upset at home or at school. But as he has the fire of the Aries and the need to develop his practical abilities, plus being as stubborn as a Horse, these inborn traits will cause him and his family a few collisions. Which will not be too major, but will show what type of a clever and inventive youngster he can develop into. And as a natural adventurous Aries/Horse persona, he will want to achieve what he thinks he can! Plus he will get very angry if he is unable to succeed in carrying out his projects which he has carefully planned. So be tolerant with this lively Aries/Horse when he gets into these self-made holes, just keep him busy at home under a watchful eye, for he is really a charming personality.

THE POSITIVE TRAITS OF THE HORSE:

In describing the Horse's positive traits these can be summed up as his ability to convince others through using his logical mind and by giving simple examples to convey his thoughts. This makes him become a popular companion, because not only is he intelligent but he is also willing to work hard, particularly when he is involved in leading others to do their best. At the same time he is a very determined person, becoming single-minded when he is after getting what he wants. He can even be accused of being selfish, which does not worry him at all, for he will say, 'I am single-minded.' And to show he has class, he is very creative in his style of dress, particularly when he wants to impress those who criticizes him. He will also become autonomous if he thinks he is not being accepted for who he is. As this belief is backed by his ability to accomplish his many projects, without the help of others. And he can do this because he has a strong internal self-discipline. Now this self-control is not common with some other year signs, so he can become a little despot if allowed, as he goes about doing what he wants.

In resume, most of these traits are mainly physical and practical, as well as being mentally stable. His major strength is that his talents are all self-controlled by his strong self-belief, which allows him to know what he wants and how to go about achieving his goals. With these strong traits, the Horse year is seen as a good addition to many of the Western zodiac sun sign. However, with the combination of the Aries sign, there could well be an initial tussle in order to settle priorities, as the former can become a little too aggressive in his demands for achieving quick results, without much planning. But this child's Horse common sense will endure, for as a sign he is far more mature than the fiery Aries. Though this youth will have to learn to control his tongue, as he can become a little blunt when he expresses his opinions about what he does not agree with.

THE NEGATIVE TRAITS OF THE HORSE:

The Horse has few weaknesses; his selfishness, which has already been stated, and he will admit he is single-minded. If you question his ideals he will rebel and get angry, because he will believe all he thinks and does is right. For this belief is part of his security blanket and helps maintain his self-esteem. By this I mean, this child will expect and count on the full support of his parents, because he tries very hard to behave correctly at home and at school. Yet at the same time, to hide his anger this Aries/Horse will get on with his work quickly, to overcome his sense of self-doubts and self-worries. Because this vulnerability will lead him to become tactless, as he defends his actions. For in his need to succeed, he will become quiet and stubborn, thinking that in this way he will be left to do as he pleases. I have to add this description is only visible on the rare occasions when this youth gets angry. For the goal of the Horse is to always become a popular personality, as this will lift his spirits and his self-importance.

In resume, this merger brings out a streak of rebellion on the part of this youth, which originates from his own idea he is not being accepted by those around him. He imagines this false impression as he knows of his natural bluntness and honest behaviors, which his family and friends will have told him about. But he can become quite dramatic about this fault, which is not that obvious. But this excuse that he is being misunderstood will be enough to give him the right to do as he pleases, in support of his claim he is not being liked. This misunderstanding leads him to blame others, if they do not agree with his strong opinions, though he will relent when it is convenient. For certainly he is no fool. As a Horse he is gifted with a logical thinking brain, which has his own particular kind of logic that leads him to become autonomous, as soon as possible to be free of parental control.

THE EARLY BEHAVIORS OF THE ARIES/HORSE:

It would seem this Aries/Horse cannot help but to be active to amuse himself. Though one thing his parents can be sure off, he will never be purposely naughty when he is busy enjoying himself. And when he is mischievous, he will use his type of self-defense tactics: being pleasant, or blaming others because they did not join him in his fun. So what else can he do? For being naughty is not his fault. With these arguments this articulate Aries/Horse lawyer has it made. Naturally his parents will have to be quite firm with him to outline his boundaries, as to what he can and cannot do. But they also have to understand he has to try to amuse himself by self-testing his many manual abilities. The best remedy to avoid him from getting into major mischief is to get involved with him as much as possible. This will stop him from inventing new games with his toys, which can lead to some upset as he can damage some of the furniture. Certainly this parental involvement will stop most problems, because he would then have been directed to do the right thing by his vigilant minders.

So this Aries/Horse child can become a challenge because of his direct forms of behaviors. The way this brave single-minded and logical young personality expresses himself is basic and direct, little thinking that he is no longer hunting for his needs. For, in this clear Aries/Horse's opinion, there is no need for discussion or negotiations regarding his needs and his wishes, for he knows how to achieve his goals, so why delay in giving them to him? He will have come to this simple conclusion as he has already thought about his needs and how to get them. So when faced with this mature, practical and mostly sensible child, many adults would wonder how someone so young can express himself so clearly as to what he needs. For this behavior is not expected from most children, who can and do become highly emotional, as they tend to cry when they express their needs when they do not get them met. But not this Aries/Horse child, who acts as if he is almost too old for his own good. Sadly or otherwise, this is his normal way of speaking; for in his busy mind he does not want to waste time, as he is already thinking what to do next to amuse himself.

THE ARIES/HORSE AS THE FIRST BORN:

But to continue, if this Aries/Horse is born the eldest in his family he would become a patronizing dictator with his siblings. But as soon as he is made aware of his forceful attitude, in the way he deals with his young ones, he would change his tack somewhat. For he is sensible enough to realize that others too have ideas of their own. And of course like him they would want to put them into practice. Happily, because of his wise, direct and logical understanding of this concept, he will accept the ideas of his siblings of what they want to do. So he would become more adaptable and easier to live with. For I have to state, at no time does this Aries/Horse youth set out to be difficult on purpose, though he can become difficult in his behaviors, when he cannot get others to quickly understand his logic. And this fact is due to his forcefulness as an Aries, plus his logical Horse's thinking patterns. However, when he is looking after his charges, he would behave very much as the protective God Father. For he would see to it that his siblings are receiving his best care and attention, because he wants to keep them safe. Sadly his strict methods might not always be appreciated by his younger brothers, who might want to do their own thing, particularly when they able to do so. However this Aries/Horse has one saving grace, in that he will be able to repair or even make new toys, and this alone will promote him as a popular big brother.

THE ARIES/HORSE AS THE SECOND CHILD:

If this Aries/Horse is born in the middle or the youngest in his family, he would try to control his brothers by using all his inborn charms. When he sees he cannot he would then try to accommodate his behaviors to the general rules. For his basic need will always be to behave in such a way to be liked by all his family. This would become his main concern to achieve his personal security blanket. This genuine need to be liked can be the first step to teach this child or youth how to behave within his family unit. The first thing he will have to learn is to become more flexible with his ideas and dictums, at least within his family's structure. For even though he can see clearly the solution to a mundane family problem, he will have to learn to wait until he has learned to express himself in a kinder mode. In this way his solutions will be accepted, not only by his family, but also by his friends and peers at school. Most people will readily recognize his logical solutions, which are clear and mostly acceptable. However, the bossy Aries/Horse youth needs to accept that ordering people about is not the best way to enlist their co-operation.

THE ARIES/HORSE ATTITUDE TOWARDS BULLIES:

One good trait inherent in this Aries/Horse is he does not like bullies among his peer group, and he will defend his weaker family members and friends in every possible way. For as an Aries/Horse he has the easy courage to stand up to adversity, and the ability to overcome difficult situations. This is one of the best traits of his Aries/Horse characteristics; the defender of the weak. As his natural passion would be to seek a solution to emotional problems by acting firmly and fairly in order to solve any immature injustice. Though he would want to be the final arbitrator if other solutions are offered. So when faced with such an impasse, the parents and teachers of this solid Aries/Horse will have to explain to this White Knight that he is not always right in his judgments or decisions. Because he is not experienced enough in his social development. Therefore, this Aries/Horse has to understand that before he can make any impulsive judgment to defend what he considers to be unfair, he has to first gather all the relevant information relating to the incident and what did happen. Plus to delay his action if he not sure of his information.

SOME ODD BEHAVIORS OF THE ARIES/HORSE:

Yet as this Aries/Horse matures from child to teenager and beyond, what can bedevil his parents is this youth's propensity to become infatuated with another student or adult around him, for no apparent reason. Sadly this is one of his weaknesses; to hero worship those he admires. When this happens, in his single mindedness he will want to follow his/her hero whenever possible. This will make him forget his work at home and at school. He will also forget his normal routines, which he is used to, and wonder about like a love-sick dog, looking around for his loved one. The best method to help him overcome this emotional hurdle is to talk with him about his emotional development, and how he has to control his 'love' for others who might not return his attention, or who might not be ready to do so because of all sorts of impediments. Certainly when he realizes his love is not being returned, and there is little he can do about it, he will get emotionally hurt. At times this let down could cause him to have negative feelings in his later life, when he is naturally looking for a solid relationship. So a sympathetic talk about his feelings, and how best to understand his admiration will do this Aries/Horse the world of good. Happily not all Aries/Horses will fall into this trap, but some will, so parents beware of this 'love bird.'

So to avoid this type of early emotional upset to happen, the one single trait this Aries/Horse should be encouraged to follow and develop is to practice his self-discipline through his academic studies and sport. His aim should be to become as educated as possible, and as physically involved in any competitive sport where he can learn to be part of a team.

These aims should be his objectives, which will form the tramlines set out by all those who care for him. As these safe guidelines will keep this fiery Aries/Horse persona on the straight and narrow. I keep repeating these ideas, because there is so much talent within this youth that he should be made aware of his full potential. Which will only be realized through his self-control and learning to protect his self-esteem. For by following a strict code of behaviors he will be able to reach his true success as a balanced personality.

It is also important for him to understand that by completing most of the projects he is involved with, this success will lead him to becoming a pillar in society, both at home and at school. This is an important habit that he should develop, because this will show his peers and teachers just how dependable he is. For as an ardent Aries/Horse personality he is a gifted doer. I therefore encourage his parents to use a little emotional blackmail on their talented child, which will go a long way to help him keep on his basic path to develop most, if not all, of his positive talents. He is intelligent enough to do well in his studies because he will be helped by his practical methods to fulfil his commitments, which are better than others who might be cleverer than him.

SUMMARY OF THE ARIES/HORSE CHARACTERISTICS AND BEHAVIOR:

☺ Energetic, warm-hearted, loyal, self-reliant, honest, endurance, reliable.

☹ Vain, stubborn, selfish, unpredictable, restless, strong-willed, intolerant .

IF THIS CHILD IS MISBEHAVING:

The Horse year is known for his logical energetic enterprises. Who is full of ideas to self-improve, but in his own way. He is warm-hearted but very independent, preferring his freedom to being held back by a loving, yet demanding family unit. He has the ability to work hard but with a sense of order, and not needing too many people around him to accomplish his tasks. He is a loyal child who still wants to be allowed to do his own thing, rather than follow well tried methods to reach a target. For he thinks he is better than the average because of his manual dexterities. The other side of him is as single-minded as his positive habits. For he can become extravagant when he is successful, vain and then stubborn when reprimanded. Being free to do what he wants is his main idea. This makes him become frank in his talk and able to blame others for his mistakes as he hates being seen as incompetent. He also likes to look smart to cover up for any of his mistakes because of his inexperience. Lastly he can become a rebel when he is frustrated when his plans do not work out.

The merger of Aries and Horse produces a child who can become a powerful personality if he has the support of his parents. He will need to be tamed from the start to obey the rules of the home, or else he will make his own laws. However, he prefers to have laws than not. But if he breaks a law he does not accept physical punishment unless he is allowed to defend himself first. When proved wrong he will accept being put in detention and stopped from enjoying his favourite past time. Using emotional blackmail on him is better than shouting at him or making him look silly. He has the pride of an adult and at times, the common sense of one. But then he can be as naïve as a junior when he is infatuated with an idea of making something out of bits of scrap. He has to learn to listen to others as he wants to be listened himself. His parents will learn a lot from him as he will have to learn a lot from them.

FAMOUS ARIES/HORSE PERSONALITIES

William Morris (24 March 1834): An English textile designer, poet, novelist, translator and revolutionary socialist. He is known for his efforts to revive the old traditional methods of textile production in Northern England; bringing back pride to the textile industry. An idealistic Aries/Horse who was successful in his practical efforts to do good for the common folk.

Dora Russell (3 April 1894): An English feminist, social activist and writer. She believed in sexual freedom and was a strong socialist campaigner, thinking that Communism was the answer to most social problems. She was wrong in practice, but right in theory, like many Aries/Horse personalities.

E. Power Biggs (29 March 1906): An English born American concert organist and recording artist. He brought listening to organ music back into popularity by playing works by all the famous pre-Romantic composers. He achieved this because of his own personal enthusiasm. A true active Aries/Horse personality.

Krome George (27 March 1918): An American businessman and former CEO of Alcoa Incorporate, Inc. He is credited as being the power behind making the company a world-leading aluminum producer. Now his company has many other interests, reaching world-wide distribution and producing diverse materials. Certainly the prototype of the ardent Aries/Horse persona who is inventive and hardworking.

Sandra Day O'Conner (26 March 1930): An American Supreme Court Judge. She was the first woman to be appointed to this post in the USA from 1981 to 2006. She deserved this huge honor in taking on such an important position, earned because of her dedicated work. A good example of a true Aries/Horse personality.

Jerome Isaac Friedman (28 March1930): An American physicist, winner of the Nobel Prize for Physics in 1990 for his research in discovering the structure of protons known a 'quarks.' He was an Emeritus Professor at the Massachusetts Institute of Technology. A position which was just right for a positive Aries/Horse.

Helmut Kohl (3 April 1930): A German chancellor and statesman from 1982 to 1998. He was also the leader of the Christian Democratic Party from 1973 to 1998, thus becoming the longest serving and active leader of West Germany's Government. He presided over the reunification of West Germany with East Germany and in 1998 was named Honorary Citizen of Europe for his work in the formation of the European Union

Spike Milligan (16 April 1930): An English comedian, poet, playwright, musician, soldier and satirist. He co-wrote the script for the very popular BBC comedy series, the Goon Show. He is regarded as one of the best comedians of the 20th Century. He used his many Aries/Horse's talents to make people happy. His life story is full of his inventive and practical successes, because he just worked hard.

Neil Kinnock (28 March 1942): An English politician and leader of the Labour Party from 1983 to 1992. The longest serving leader of the opposition, later he became Vice President to the European Commission. He is honored as a straight speaking, honest personality who can get things done.

Daniel C. Dennett (28 March 1942): An American philosopher, writer and cognitive scientist whose research centers on the philosophy of the mind and the study of science; particularly of biology. He was awarded the Jean Nicod Prize and the Erasmus Prize in 2012, which he richly deserved.

Jackie Chan (7 April 1954): A Chinese actor, martial arts expert, singer and stunt performer. He developed his own style of martial arts by blending it with physical comedy, which became a very popular mix. This clever mix of serious and fun martial arts not only served to entertain, but also motivated people to learn this highly disciplined exercise.

Samantha Fox (15 April 1966): An English actress, glamour model and pop star. A popular 'pin-up'' girl in the English press during the 1980s, she also achieved fame as a singer and has sold over 30 million albums.

Trine Hattested (18 April 1966): A Norwegian javelin thrower and international athlete who represented her country for many years. She won many sporting competitions and was well liked by most other athletes because she was straight and fair, plus determined to win fairly. A true Aries/Horse persona.

Jaime Alguersuari (23 March 1990): a Spanish retired racing driver best known for competing in Formula One between 2009 and 2011, and for being the 2008 British Formula Three champion. He became the youngest Formula One driver in history to start a Grand Prix at the 2009 Hungarian Grand Prix – at the age of 19 years. His driving skills and cool tactics prove that these traits are normal for a true Aries/Horse personality.

CHAPTER 8

ARIES/GOAT

THE ARIES/GOAT PERSONALITY

If ever there is a contradictory set of inborn traits arising from the merger of any two astrological birth signs, then the Aries/Goat can safely be said to be one of the most awkward combinations. The one theory which mitigates this combination is the belief, 'we all choose our birth signs.' And in this case we better believe it! Obviously I now have to explain this disturbing initial tough statement, so that you can make some sense of what I have written. However I have enough proof to support my opinion, just by describing the different traits inborn in each of these birth signs. So I start by describing the Aries personality who is so different from that of the Goat. For the former can become aggressive if he gets angry, and the latter would rather keep quiet, but will show his aggression in hidden ways. Then the Aries is a primitive, brave hunter, while the Goat prefers to be led, protected and provided for, without getting too involved in any proactive action.

These can be said to be exaggerations of inborn traits, but I use them to prove my theory. Though the important aspect of this merger is that these disparate inborn traits do eventually fuse to form an intelligent, inventive personality. And the proof of this claim is at the end of this personality description where I list different famous personalities who were all born during the time of the Aries month and the Goat year. But to highlight the main differences between these signs: Aries is very much, 'I am important and so I am willful' and the Goat is quite the opposite, 'I want to be looked after, so I shall obey the rules I agree with.' So the former is the basic leader, and the latter is mainly an obedient follower! Naturally the resulting merger of these very different attitudes produces quite a complex persona. Because at times he will show he has strong opinions, yet in others he will be a slippery individual, for the very inventive ways they create to reach his ends, without causing any major waves.

THE POSITIVE TRAITS OF THE GOAT:

The positive traits of the Goat are very different to those of the Aries. For this Chinese Goat's personality is so sensitive he can be termed as being shy, or timid and even nebulous when compared with our stronger Capricorn Goat. One can only hope that all the Aries positive traits and abilities will become a support to those of Goat's positive traits, which are very light but useful. The Goat is in fact very inventive, and creative, as he is very intelligent. This creativity is backed by his perseverance, which will get him to work very hard if he has to. For once he gets interested in any subject or task he will keep at it, until he is satisfied with what he is doing. Plus he has done all he wants to do with his initiative. Happily for this Goat he is also aware that he has an odd and complex personality. So to hide his complexity he will develop a strategy for demonstrating a wide range of good manners, with a charming disposition, which most people do not bother to exhibit.

He will use these gentle behaviors to protect his fragile self-esteem, which he will then enhance with a show of good taste. Though all these traits show this Goat's personality to be seen as a tame or an easy going persona, with the impression that he is easy to influence, the reality is that he is not so easy to dominate and he has a strong self-loving core based on his survival instincts and evasive skills. These he will demonstrate when he gets into a temper, for still waters run deep, and his self-love runs even deeper. In short, one can say, if well nurtured at home the Aries/Goat can be seen as an embryonic genius. Because there is the forceful but logical intelligence of the Aries, plus the creativity of the inventive Goat. Which when welded together, with tender but firmly led constant understanding, will produce a child/youth with enough controlled energies to do very well for himself.

THE NEGATIVE TRAITS OF THE GOAT:

The Goat for his part shares his negative traits with those of Aries, which are his lack of foresight, which makes him have an impracticable attitude in the way he starts his work, as he tends to start and then stop. This hesitance makes him fail some of his tasks, because he is not too sure of his end results. And when he does fail, he becomes pessimistic about his abilities and what he will do in the future. Though this is not the usual Goat's ending, because he will work hard to self-improve. But to avoid further stress by doing difficult work, he will try to do the least possible, so as not to look bad and give himself further worries. Lastly, and certainly while he is young, because of his sensitive self-doubts he is in constant worry about some situations where he foresees he cannot control to his satisfaction. Sadly this feeling of being vulnerable makes him very uncomfortable in circumstances which he gauges are beyond his capabilities to defend himself.

In resume, the combination of all these inborn different negative traits add up to producing a personality who is mostly unsure of himself, and who is constantly grasping for support. But on the flip side, this child could become a very creative persona, who is also very inventive some of the time, when he sees an opportunity to shine. The only sad part in this description is that all these negative traits are imbedded in this sign, because he is so very sensitive. This fact makes him fear making mistakes, as this possibility upsets his peace of mind, so he ends up by doing as little as possible. Now this reads dire, but these descriptions are a brief resume of this sign's inborn hidden negative traits, but they do not become apparent immediately, or all at once. Happily for this Goat he is a good actor, as he has had to learn to hide his weaknesses with a shyness and sensitivity, which will melt anyone's heart.

THE EARLY BEHAVIORS OF THE ARIES/GOAT CHILD/YOUTH:

After the initial personal descriptions I have written regarding the Aries and the Goat year, one can begin to understand and imagine the difference in the personal traits of these two birth signs; Aries is the pioneer and out front, the Goat wants to hide. But happily, when you take a closer look and study these two very different sets of traits, you will discover that there can be a very positive end result if this child/youth is helped to develop his positive traits and control his weaker ones. However the end results of this merger can be deceptive, for at times this child will take his steps forwards into the unknown with strength and panache, to succeed in doing what he has set out to do. But then when challenged as to what he is doing, he will fade away and almost hide. This change of attitude will cause him and those around him some sort of vague frustration, even anger, but his parents or his teachers will know that this Aries/Goat child can do what he has to do without any problem. But yet at other times he will hesitate so as not to make mistakes. Then there will be other times when he will come forward with a temper, which can/ will erase anyone's doubt over whether he can be seen as incompetent.

At home when young this Aries/Goat child will certainly show he is very sensitive, followed by an attitude of lack of determination, or strength of purpose. Then if he is accused that he's not doing his best, he would turn round and defend himself, with a bravado which will out do any ordinary fighting Lawyer. Now this conflict between opposite behaviors is a permanent feature in this child's character. But the best way to help him is not to point out his conflicting moods, but to offer him all the support he may need, when he needs it, by explaining the reasons for his bewildering actions. I believe this child is intelligent enough to hear and understand the reasons for his conflicting birth signs, and to accept his strengths and his weaknesses. However, when telling him about his weaknesses, try not to blame him for his alternating behaviors, rather instead suggest he can self-control his emotions before getting into a fight or escaping from one. For I believe telling him he has a very strong survival instinct should help him know he is not a weakling, just confused because of his contesting birth signs.

THE ARIES/GOAT AS THE FIRST BORN:

Now if this Aries/Goat is born the eldest in his family he would show his intelligence and his sensitivity, with a desire for helping his younger siblings. But he would need direction from his parents on how best to perform his leadership duties. He might even need more support in his actual practice of being a leader than expected. However, he has an advantage over other types of leaders because he is so very sensitive and instinctive that he can foresee dangerous situations, which others may be unable to perceive. This type of safety radar is one of his many positive talents, for he has a wealth of intuitive abilities, all to be used for the benefit of himself and others. Particularly when he has to protect those who are under his care. Though, in his role of being the leader he will have two distinct variations: he will demand complete authority over his charges in what they can do and how to enjoy themselves, or he might just allow them to do as they wish, blaming them if anything was to go wrong.

THE ARIES/GOAT AS THE SECOND CHILD:

If this Aries/Goat is born in the middle or the youngest in his family, his behaviors would swing from being proactive to inactive, even in his need to claim some form of protection. Added to this he would expect his elder brothers or sisters to help him out, plus to look after him when he feels unsure. By helping him I mean, doing his share of the house work, homework and indeed with any task which he finds challenging. The pity is that he is well able to do all these things for himself, but it is far easier for him to just play dumb, and have annoying tasks done for him. I have to state that at no time is this Aries/Goat a dumb-ass, just a very cunning one! Though he will however pay for this manipulation and sensitivity, as he will suffer if there is any emotional upset in the home. Because he will fear for his security which could be jeopardized by any unsteady behaviors of his elders when they are not getting on with each other. Also, if he finds any one of his siblings is receiving more attention than himself, this affection will make him feel rejected. So his reaction to this jealousy will make him tease his brother as many times as he can, just to get even.

THE SECURITY NEEDS OF THE ARIES/GOAT:

Yet there is one aspect in this Aries/Goat's life which is most important for him, and this is his need to live in a steady home environment. As this is the dream of every Aries/Goat personality. For this family steadiness would provide him with his sense of security, as well as to guarantee him that he will not be abandoned by them. In fact, this feeling of being protected is the number one requirement for this child, particularly while he is still young. For as an Aries/Goat persona he will need to feel safe and protected before he can function as an ordinary member of his community. The surprising thing is that inherently this child/youth is not a fearful persona at all. He is just full of self-doubts, though once these doubts have been erased he can act as expected, just like any other ordinary youth.

Now this feeling that he is safe within his family will strengthen his security blanket, which in his case is having the complete support of his parents and which he will believe he has richly earned because he has tried very hard to be obedient, and by being proactive he will be seen as a positive member of his family. This will mean to him that his parents do understand and support him when he is feeling vulnerable. Likewise, as a student he will feel safe when he is appreciated with the backing of his teachers. For with their support there is very little this eager Aries/Goat will not try to achieve to please them. Because getting on with his school work would be no big problem or hardship for him as he can be very creative in his learning. Also he has the ability to appear weak when it suits him, plus have the knack to have others do things for him, when in fact he could easily do them for himself.

At other times however, when this Aries/Goat is feeling pleased with himself, he will take off and work non-stop on any of his many fancy projects, until he has completed it. This project could involve working on a mammoth task, which would floor others, but would become just a personal challenge for him to prove his self-worth. I strongly suggest that when his parents and/or teachers realize this Aries/Goat has entered a period of all work and no play, they should step in and rescue him from total exhaustion. For he has to learn for his own health to pace himself. Which will mean that he has to take a rest or a break from his work to regain his lost energies. Then he can continue working until the task is completed. However, learning this habit has to be done in stages, for there is every chance that after taking a rest this Aries/Goat might not restart where he left off. Because he might well try to improve his original design and start all over again. Naturally this does not happen too often, but there is a chance he will need to learn this type of self-discipline and thereby regulate the time he spends working on any one topic, without the need for restarting it to improve it as he goes on.

The above paragraph reads a little daunting, but there are good times to be had with this inventive Aries/Goat. For during the times of social gatherings this young person can give an outward impression he is having a great time, being full of smiles and jokes. But this is done mostly to keep up appearances, so as not to rub people the wrong way, and so avoid showing his more negative side. This is a telling trait with this type of child; for he knows he can be annoying at times, so he tries very hard to act in a very sociable way, particularly when he is among other young people. For certainly he wants to impress those around him, to become popular with his peers, as he knows he is more vulnerable than he wants to project. This survival skill of pretending his bravery makes him a good actor, for believe it or not, this Aries/Goat has the makings for becoming a great actor.

THE ARIES/GOAT AS AN ACTOR:

The talent the Aries/Goat has to be able to act convincingly when he wants can be put to good use when he is feeling vulnerable. As this ability to 'fake it to make it' can give him a strong backing to feel good about himself. For while he is acting he is doing just fine; fooling himself and others will help him with his daily need to survive as it will give him a veneer of self-confidence, which will hide his self-doubts. Now this type of behavior epitomizes this youth's variations of character, because it can hide his constant feeling of being vulnerable, in a world he can hardly understand. Particularly when he is attempting to do something new which is a daring activity he has not done before. So through his controlled acting, and limiting himself to do what he can do as perfectly as possible, this Aries/Goat will gain the recognition of being a good student or class comedian. Happily, with this approved badge, this will give him the self-confidence to improve his make belief lifestyle even further. Which (if he can get away with it) would be easy for him. Plus being seen as a popular figure will help his Aries half to feel powerful and so increase his self-belief, meaning that he can go ahead to become even more daring!

THE POSITIVE TRAITS OF THE MATURE ARIES/GOAT:

Up to now I have stressed this Aries/Goat's more negative traits, but he has some very good ones, like his loyalty towards his parents, friends and teachers. This feeling of being supported by them would make him feel happy and safe, as he receives their reciprocal love he has for them. For if at any time he has to sacrifice his own pleasures, to please his family or friends he would do so, without a selfish thought. In fact, he would become a human dynamo in order to solve any pending problem which could beset his loved ones. This attitude of self-sacrifice for his family and friends is most gratifying to watch, and should be admired. And not only that, he should be praised for his unselfish efforts to put his family first. This praise would indeed do his self-love (and therefore his ego) a world of good, for it would build-up his self-esteem and help to increase his self-confidence. By now the reader will have noticed I have repeatedly pointed out the need to build up this Aries/Goats self-esteem, which will help him to overcome his feeling of not being good enough. And this fear arises from the fact that he doubts himself for most of the time, because he does not want to make mistakes. So once this self-imposed limitation of self-doubt is subdued, or overcome completely, this new era will help this Aries/Goat to get on with his life as expected.

THE ARIES/GOAT AS A SPORTS PERSON:

I have not mentioned the sporting abilities of this Aries/Goat youth, which can be very mixed. This is stated because it depends on which of his birth signs becomes more predominant in his maturing. If it is his Aries half, then this child will enjoy all types of sport and become proficient in at least a few. But if it is his Goat's half which dominates, he would enjoy watching sport rather than partaking in it. This hesitancy in getting involved in any active sport is because his Goat half will not want to look foolish in front of his peers, as he will not want to get hurt or fail. So to avoid looking silly or getting hurt, this Aries/Goat will not be too ready to take on an active part in any contact game. He will prefer to create music, art or other more intellectual activities, and not get too involved in the physical challenge of fierce competition. However when it comes to his academic achievements, if this Aries/Goat is feeling secure then he will do very well indeed. Particularly with his creative work, like his art and drama lessons or writing, indeed any work which needs any form of creative thinking. In my view this type of youth should continue his academic studies as far as possible, because he has all the ingredients to become an advanced thinker.

SUMMARY OF THE ARIES/GOAT CHARACTERISTICS AND BEHAVIOR:

☺ Perseverant, eloquent, honest, creative, ambitious, tactful, friendly, open.

☹ Lazy, stubborn, vague, touchy, moody, unpredictable, prideful.

IF THIS CHILD IS MISBEHAVING:

This child is kind and straightforward, and very eloquent when he wants to impress. He is a creative, sensitive soul who will persevere to achieve his goals. While he will work hard when pushed to do so, he can also be lazy and easily get stressed, particularly if things aren't working out the way he wants. The other side of this vague child is a huge challenge to his self-loving senses. He can be timid one moment and fierce the next, with a hidden temper which can go to extremes. This child is active and energetic, and good at defending himself. But sometimes he will need silence and calm, and to be alone with himself so that he can think things through slowly. He is a loyal member of his family, though will prefer to be fed than go out there to earn his keep. Yet when the time is right he will emerge a near genius. Indeed this combination is a complex one.

The merger of these very different birth signs produces a complex personality who will need pushing to do what he doesn't like, yet restraining when he wants to do his own thing. So at times he will become aggressive to do what he wants and will need a very firm hand. Though he will calm down once his parents show they are stronger than him. His worst fault is that he will tend to skive off doing anything he finds difficult. Here is when his parents and teachers must be adamant that he has to do what he has been told. Being a superb actor he will try his hardest to convince them he is doing his best. Most of all, he has to be made to understand that it is his duty to contribute to his own future development, with the help of his parents/teachers, and not the other way round. The parents of this Aries/Goat have a challenge; they have to be strong to make their offspring even stronger.

FAMOUS ARIES/GOAT PERSONALITIES

Daniel Bovet (23 March 1907): A Swiss born Italian pharmacologist who won the 1957 Nobel Prize in Physiology or Medicine. He discovered a drug which blocks the action of specific neurotransmitters, which helps people to lead better lives. His life story depicts most, if not all the traits of the Aries/Goat personality.

Robert Heilbroner (24 March 1919): An American economist, author and historian of economic thought. He authored over 20 books, all of which were lively and provocative and which inspired generations of students with the drama of how the world earns, or fails to earn, its living and making him one of his profession's all-time best-selling authors.

Ram Dass (born Richard Alpert) (6 April 1931): an American spiritual teacher, former academic and clinical psychologist, and author. In 1967 he traveled to India where he met his guru, Neem Karoli Baba, who gave Ram Dass his name, which means 'servant of God.' He became a pivotal influence on a culture that has reverberated with the words 'Be Here Now' ever since. He is a good prototype for the Aries/Goat personality, who wants to help those who live in fear by showing them 'the way out' and so onto self-fulfillment.

John Major (29 March 1943): An English Conservative Party politician, now an ex-Prime Minister who governed from 1990 to 1997. He was the last Conservative leader to win an outright majority at a General Election.

Vangelis (29 March 1943): A Greek musician, conductor and jazz player, who is well known for his progressive electronic music. He is best known for his film track 'Chariots of Fire.' His career has spanned over 50 years and he is one of the best creators of electronic music – very much the area of the Aries/Goat's preference.

Hector Oliver (5 April 1943): An Argentinean film director and producer, internationally well known for his provocative films. He enjoys directing political films, giving his version of real events, but not always as politicians may want events portrayed.

Ann Meyers (26 March 1955): An American basketball player turned analyst for the N.B.C. sports coverage of Women's Basketball League Games. While at college she scored more points than any other player, male or female. Her Aries strength and Goat's creativity give her the ability to reach success.

Reba McEntire (28 March 1955): An American country singer, songwriter and actress. While singing the National Anthem at a local rodeo she caught the ear of a Mercury Records scout. She has released 26 studio albums and over 40 singles.

Frederick Ryan Jr. (12 April 1955): An American Chief of Staff for the former USA President Ronald Reagan 1989/95. He is currently serving as the Chairman of the Board of Trustees for the Ronald Reagan Foundation. He is also CEO and President for the Politico group.

Dodi Al Fayed (15 April 1955): An Egyptian businessman and boyfriend of Princess Diana, with whom he died in a tragic car crash in Paris on August 31st 1997. The accident has been investigated in depth by various police teams to try and discover the true cause and reason for the crash.

John Ziegler (28 March 1967): An American radio program host, documentary film writer/director and journalist. He is known to be a controversial conservative commentator and columnist and has appeared as a guest on nearly every major television talk show. In 2008 he co-produced, wrote and directed a provocative documentary entitled 'Blocking the Path to 9/11.'

Troy Gentry (5 April 1967): An American country singer who purchased a black bear from a wildlife facility and subsequently shot the bear from inside an electrified enclosure, a practice commonly known as 'canned hunting'. He pleaded guilty to a charge of falsely tagging a bear as if it had been killed in the wild and agreed to pay a $15,000 fine. Gentry apologized for his actions as well as the unethical manner in which he killed the bear. His actions are too weird for words, as are some of the Aries/Goat's most daring deeds.

Dara Torres (15 April 1967): An American swimmer and Olympic medalist. She is also a mother, TV personality and motivational speaker. In 2005 she was inducted into the Jewish Hall of Fame as the winner of 4 Gold, 3 Silver and 4 Bronze medals, all collected during her sporting involvements during 5 Olympic Games!

Rachel Corrie (10 March 1979): An American activist and pro-Palestinian supporter, she was killed while trying to block an Israeli armored bulldozer as she defended the demolition of a Palestinian home. The exact nature of her death remains surrounded with controversy with fellow protestors saying that the Israeli soldier operating the bulldozer deliberately ran over her, and others saying that it was an accident since the bulldozer operator could not see her. The sad part of the Aries/Goat's personality; brave and sentimental, but not always understood.

CHAPTER 9

ARIES/MONKEY

THE ARIES/MONKEY PERSONALITY

This combination of birth signs will make this Aries child feel happy through this proactive and attractive merger. For a union with the clever Monkey is a very exciting merger indeed for any birth sign. Because the Aries/Monkey union remains true to the traditional Aries characteristics, this helps the Aries to become freer than with other Chinese year signs. And as a plus, by being blessed in merging with a personality who is funny, cunning, and as smart as any true Monkey, this fusion makes this quick and powerful merger into an exciting one.

As whatever this intrepid Aries/Monkey wants, he will normally achieve by the smoothest of ways. In resume, there is little this child/youth cannot do which will not lead him to his inborn eventual success. Because he has that magical ability which helps him have second sight, or a sense that he can see 'around corners.' This unique talent gives him the gift to foresee what is needed to achieve his objectives. Added to this, he has the panache of the Aries and the swift, bright cunningness of the Monkey. Making this a superb, bright individual.

These natural gifts give this child an in-depth self-confidence, even while he is still young, which is usually reached by more mature children. So reading these statements makes one believe these Aries/Monkey people are indeed very lucky. Though they have to be taught to develop a firm and strong self-discipline, or else their luck will change into disaster! So in total, if this child is brought up in a normal, balanced and well organized home environment, he has every chance to become a star wherever he goes. For, not only is this child full of energy as an Aries, but he will also be full of the guile and clever tactics of the Monkey, who is able to get on with most people. Therefore this combination should help this child/youth get all the necessary help he will need in his future life.

I also have to admit this child/youth will obviously be born with some selfish negative traits, which will balance all his inborn positive ones. But by and large, this Aries born Monkey will become a very active and pleasant young person, who will want to have his way by hook or by crook! For he has the audacity of the Aries to succeed, plus the cunningness of the agile Monkey to achieve what he wants. In my assessment of the 144 double birth signs, a better union will be hard to find.

THE POSITIVE TRAITS OF THE MONKEY:

He is naturally a cunning individual, who is mostly full of innovative thinking. This ability helps him solve many young people's mundane problems easily, as he seems to know the root of most 'childish' problems. This cleverness helps him to be full of improvisations, helping him find ways and means on how best to reach his aims. And he will do this by using simple, direct and effective tactics, because he does not fall into the trap of getting emotional involved in reaching for his needs. For he can wait and foresee his clear opportunities. Then he will take the necessary action to succeed, without getting into too much of a hassle.

Naturally this type of behavior makes him became a very sensible leader. Though he will only take command of any situation when there is no other recourse. Finally he is able to influence others by his use of his famous wit, which is unaffected by any stray show of other peoples weak emotions, or his ego, just to prove his one-upmanship. For this Monkey is normally self-confident enough to keep his self-esteem under control, until he needs it, to clearly demonstrate he is no fool. Now all these traits are based on his intellectual skills, to work out the best way to achieve his personal successes. He can also add to these tactics, the advantage of only using the minimum of his own selfish energies. And to cap it all, he is also able to acquire sufficient practical manual skills to become an excellent handy man.

THE NEGATIVE TRAITS OF THE MONKEY:

The Monkey's weaknesses are his sly cunningness and self-seeking pleasures, because he believes in looking after himself first! This leads him to becoming deceitful if necessary, and to cover up for his faults he can become plain silly, as a decoy for his clever manipulations. He also has the ability to seize any opportunity to do as he wishes, without getting into trouble. And as he is full of ruse, he is perceptive enough to notice discrepancies in any arguments he listens to from his parents. Then he will become cheeky with his own observations of their behaviors, which will annoy them, but mostly he will be correct in his assessments.

But in retrospect, what this bright child/youth says has more than a grain of common sense in it. One therefore has to admit this Monkey has a mature way of thinking and this, added to the simple logic of the daring Aries, creates a fusion that will help make him become a powerful personality. Particularly when it comes to becoming a proactive leader of any group. As he can perceive the future with a very clear vision. Now I have to disclaim that all Aries/Monkeys are going to be this smart, but in my experience many of them are!

THE EARLY BEHAVIORS OF THE ARIES/MONKEY CHILD/YOUTH:

In resume, when taking this merger as a whole it produces a personality who can be called a 'high octane child.' It means therefore his parents and teachers will have to keep him busy with a rich variety of set tasks, all to be completed as expected, to the highest level possible. This is the one suggestion I can make; always demand from this child/youth his best efforts, because he can. And he has to be told that any other lower result is not acceptable. The reason to state this is quite simple, this child knows he is intelligent, therefore in most cases he will try to get away with it by doing the minimum. As is normal with most children who are more interested in doing what they want to do, rather than what they have to do.

But when this brave Aries, plus clever Monkey youth knows this selfish ploy is not allowed, he will get used to performing at his normal high level of attainment. Because of this fact, I recommend during his early years that this astute Aries/Monkey child should follow a strict set of work and behavior rules, both at home and at school. This strategy should train him to get used to developing his own type of self-discipline, to do his best for his own good. For I firmly believe without a strong core of self-control, most if not all of his powerful traits would dissipate and become weakened, even become 'wishy-washy.' This neglect would be a great pity, for there is so much potential packed inside this individual that any failure would do him no good, or the rest of his family. I state this because I know of a few Aries/Monkeys who have wasted their potential as individuals due to their lack of stamina to become real stars. For to develop their full potential they need the firm challenge to survive, to reach for and do their best, rather than just to drift along, simply because they can.

THE FOLLY OF AN ARIES/MONKEY CHILD/YOUTH WITHOUT DIRECTION:

On another matter, as this Aries/Monkey youth is hard to fool, because he is clever and quick on the up take, this child needs to feel he is being looked after and educated to the best of the abilities of his parents and teachers. Other than that, he would just play about; waste his time and that of those in his family. Because he would assume, 'They don't care what I do.' So the best solution is to keep him busy doing practical activities, with a definite objective in view, or else he will keep his family busy by not always doing the correct thing.

Though he would be careful not to do anything too drastic, so as not to get punished. But there is every chance he could become annoying, as he goes about inventing his self-made tests, to create his adventures, which will help him discover his limits. Even when he is within his own peer group he could go over the top with his pranks and jokes, just to prove how clever he is. Now these are not malicious accusations made about the negative potential inborn in this active Aries/Monkey youth. But what can happen if this youth is allowed to run wild. For my aim is to describe his normal behaviors, as an active, agile, clever and daring adventurous little monkey, with time on his hands.

THE ARIES/MONKEY AS THE FIRST BORN:

If this Aries/Monkey is born the eldest in his family, he should be encouraged to become an example for the rest of his brothers and sisters. Mostly because of his common sense, he should try to keep the house rules and the peace at home. But there is always the chance that at any time he might take off and do something silly, just to impress his followers with his many abilities to be inventive. Though he will always have a really good reason to explain why he did what he did.

I compare this Aries/Monkey youth's vitality and activities to a stick of dynamite. It can be used for a good cause, such as being used to make tunnels, splitting hard rock with its explosive energy. Or this energy can be used just to blow up things, for no other reason than to be destructive because he is aimless. Though I have to state clearly, this youth will not normally set out to cause trouble or harm anyone. Though he could cause some upsets within his close family, simply because he will try to discover his outer limits through his own self-testing, if he is allowed too much personal freedom. So I recommend this first-born Aries/Monkey youth is made to understand his many responsibilities when he is in charge of his naive younger siblings. For he has to realize the power and control he can exercise over their behaviors.

THE ARIES/MONKEY AS THE SECOND CHILD:

Now if this Aries/Monkey is born in the middle or the youngest in the family, his parents and his older siblings should demand sensible behaviors from him, at least for most of the time. With no funny business or monkey tricks, which will rock the boat at home. Though at the same time the rest of his family would have to be prepared to become his audience, 'to keep the peace' when he has some funny scenes to act out in front of them. Possibly he would have worked on these funny sketches in his own time while he had been sent to his room to cool down, after one of his many audacious tricks. For one can hardly blame him, coming up with some interesting story to entertain himself 'while in the cooler' which he will want to share with the rest of his family.

And this is because with his vivid and active imagination this Aries/ Monkey will not like wasting time while he is in solitary. For he would be thinking up some sort of drama to make his imposed time-out pass quicker. So my suggestion is to separate him from the rest of his family's activities when he has acted in a selfish manner. In this way its teaching him he has to learn to develop his own self-control. For this form of detention will teach him he has to be aware of the negative consequences of his unthinking silly actions. I can confirm this firm strategy does work, for this young Aries/Monkey does not like being alone, unless it is his own choice.

RECOMMENDATION FOR THE NURTURING OF THE ARIES/MONKEY:

Now the reason for my advising to be very firm with this Aries/Monkey is because this youth needs to be active, but in a constructive way. For once he gets started he cannot easily be stopped because his energies are focused on his enjoyment, as this is very much part of his inborn character to be inquisitive in his self-discoveries. So he has to be guided with strict and constant directions, in order for him to use his nervous energy in doing things which are proactive and beneficial, for himself and others. For by using these simple, no nonsense type of tactics, he will know he has to conform to his family's law and order dictums. This does not mean this lively Aries/Monkey needs be treated harshly to tame him, for he will still need as much loving attention as anyone else. But in his case, these firm family rules which have clear cut boundaries, will help to contain him and at the same time serve to protect him from getting into unforeseen troubles.

This is not to say this Aries/Monkey should not be given some leeway to develop his funnier side. For he will always be ready to provide some light relief, when the family is in some sort of emotional tension. So not all his honest critical comments about his family should be seen as annoying. Because in his quick thinking brain, as an Aries, merging with the cool logical judgments of the Monkey, this youth can reason far beyond the norm of most people's capacity. As this inborn ability to analyses stressful situations and their solutions is a talent which should be encouraged in this alert youth as soon as it becomes evident.

But for all his cleverness, this Aries/Monkey has still to obey the guidelines as outlined by his parents. For these rules should commit him to following the norms at home and at school, and certainly help him to stay out of trouble. And when he does abide by the rules, he should be given some sort of privilege, or earned Kudos to encourage him to keep up the good work. Plus more than this, he should be praised and made an example of so that others try and emulate his positive contribution to keep the peace within the family. For, as a good actor, this Aries/Monkey can enjoy the limelight because of his better behaviors, rather than his examples of negative ones. This alert youth will realize that by abiding to most of the home rules he is able to gain more freedom than when he plays about out of control. So by keeping his wild energies under control this Aries/Monkey will gain far more than just the freedom he needs to perform his self-testing.

Now all I have suggested is to help control this Aries/Monkey youth, but his parents will still have to be very much involved with their child's upbringing otherwise he could cause them some mischief. As without a firm and direct set of family guidance rules, this selfish youth will miss out on how to behave within the structure of a family group. This will provide him with the basic role model to follow when he creates his own family. And to motivate him to follow these rules, he should be led to believe that these formal guidelines are like a test or challenge to increase his own self-esteem and self-control. Which should motivate him to continue with his self-improvement efforts, as they keep him out of trouble and gain him the acknowledgement from his family or teachers that his good work is being noticed and appreciated.

THE ARIES/MONKEY AT SCHOOL:

At school this Aries/Monkey should have no difficulty in finishing his work quickly. And after being told to check his work through, his teacher should encourage him to give a helping hand to slower students. This responsibility should have a calming effect on him, as he would like to be seen as dependable. Plus this privilege would also help him to keep the peace in class, and so avoid him becoming a bother if he has nothing else to do. Added to this sense of self-worth this Aries/Monkey would feel he has gained some status among his fellow students, apart from providing some comic relief at times.

However as a safety valve, his teacher should allow this youth to play the clown, perhaps during his drama lessons, by being original in his caricatures. Though his drama teacher has to insist that he shouldn't expect to play to the gallery all of the time. But this opportunity to act would give this Aries/Monkey the opportunity to show how talented he is. Particularly as an acute observer who does not miss any odd yet funny scenes in the classroom. For he will love to give his own version of what is funny, at what we call 'the ordinary life events we take for granted.' But at the same time he will also notice what is not so funny, even down right negative behaviors in others He will understand the trouble they can cause and copy the scenes he's witnessed if it is to his own advantage. Needless to say, this Aries/Monkey youth is a potent actor, with an eye to what we can call, 'selfish behaviors,' when they are judged with a mature mind.

THE GENERAL BEHAVIORS OF THE ARIES/MONKEY AT HOME:

In resume, in describing the Aries/Monkey youth we have a family member and student who can act in extreme ways according to how he is treated. So at home he will abide by what is expected of him, if he is treated with the respect he feels he is owed. Likewise at school he will do his best, if he is expected to do so. For as a student he will do his best if motivated to do so for his own good. As he is quite selfish in his self-love, which can be used as leverage to get him to work hard at self-improvement. Both in the classroom and on the playing fields. In fact as an athlete he has all the ingredients to do very well, particularly in individual sports where he does not depend on others to fulfill his need to shine. To me the most important aspect of his nurturing is he is kept busy for most of the time. To be involved in activities which will enhance his personality, and away from other habits which will endanger his health. For as he matures he will want to try all sort of experiments, to discover his mental capacities and enter the hidden world of the psychic mind. I believe in motivating this youth to join activity clubs for organized games and/or individual pursuits. From football to gymnastics, cycling to boxing, essentially any type of activity which will stimulate his risk-taking traits and challenges him to discover his limits.

☺ Clever, inventive, charming, eloquent, energetic, enthusiastic, cheerful.

☹ Impetuous, selfish, opportunistic, manipulative, opinionated, fearless, erratic.

IF THIS CHILD IS MISBEHAVING:

This is a clever child full of intelligence and eloquence. His best traits are that he can be flexible, charming, enthusiastic and courageous. On a good day he can be brilliant in his actions. Yet he wants to be independent to achieve quick success in whatever he attempts. At times he is impetuous and helpful. At others, he is just selfish and ready to be an opportunist to reach his targets. This combination can result in a child that wants everything from life all at once, but they quickly become tired and start to get bored. Such an eccentricity can prevent them from succeeding. On a bad day this child can be too clever for his own good – enough to annoy his family and friends. He is an ace Machiavellian; devious and cunning in using tricks to fool others. He can be impatient and easily frustrated by slower peers who are preventing him from getting what or where he wants. He can use his own version of the truth when it suits him.

The merger of these positive birth signs will make it a challenge for his parents/teachers. Telling this child what to do does not mean he will do it. So a very firm hand is needed. Hence to overcome his clever tactics, stop him from doing the things he likes to do. Talk to him about his responsibilities to himself and to his family. Use every type of emotional blackmail and even detentions, to make him realize that being cunning is not the way to make his mark at home, school or beyond. Therefore he must know that his parents and teacher will be after him to do his duties. In fact, he will not mind this strict upbringing, for in the wild he will lose his chances of advancing in the right direction. It is best to talk to him at eye level, but there are times he just needs to be told, or else. Again, though he wants to be free, he needs to come home to a firm household. He is in fact a paradox personality, so he has to be treated as one.

FAMOUS ARIES/MONKEY PERSONALITIES:

Leonardo da Vinci (15 April 1452): An Italian artist, sculptor, architect and inventor. He is recognized as a genius and considered to be one of the most influential artists of all times and whose areas of interest included science, music, mathematics, engineering, anatomy, geology, astronomy, botany and cartography. Widely considered one of the most diversely talented individuals ever to have lived, he is sometimes credited with the inventions of the parachute, helicopter and tank.

Rene Descartes (31 March 1556): A French scientist, thinker, philosopher and mathematician. He is famous for his work in mathematics and analytical geometry. He is considered to be the father of modern mathematics, and by thinking 'outside of the box' he did discover the answers to many traditional questions.

James Ensor (13 April 1860): A Belgium painter and printmaker whose works are known for their bizarre fantasy and sardonic social commentary. He is famous for his surrealistic and expressionist paintings. He had a strong influence on his contemporaries, urging them to break new grounds, express their inner feelings and paint their emotions.

Bette Davis (5 April 1908): An American actress of film, TV and theater. She was regarded as one of the great actresses in Hollywood history. She was noted for her willingness to play the villain and unsympathetic, sardonic characters. Known for her forceful and intense style, she was married four times and admitted that her acting success had often been at the expense of her personal relationships.

Thomas Szasz (15 April 1920): A Hungarian/American psychiatrist. He had a very different belief regarding mental illnesses, which he said should not be seen as a medical problem, but as a problem in living styles. He was highly honored and received the title of Humanist of the Year in 1973.

Ted Morgan (30 March 1932): A French/American writer, biographer, historian and journalist. He lived a double life; one as a student at Yale University and the other as a reluctant French aristocrat. He wrote honest accounts related to the French Army's atrocities during the Algerian war. For he wanted to be honest in his search for the truth. With this he shows his true Aries/Monkey character.

Diana Ross (26 March 1944): An American singer who rose to fame as the lead singer of the vocal group the Supremes, becoming Motown's most successful act and the best charting girl group in US history. The group rivaled the Beatles in popularity and record sales. As a solo artist, she is reputed to be the most successful female singer of all times with 70 single hits and over 100 million records sold. Her life story reads like the prototype of the successful Aries/Monkey artist.

James Heckman (19 April 1944): An American economist he is a Distinguished Henry Schultz Service Professor of Economics at the Chicago University. In 2000 Heckman shared the Nobel Prize in Economic Sciences with Daniel McFadden, for his pioneering work in econometrics and microeconomics. He is among the most influential economists in the world. Easy for an Aries/Monkey to be seen as the best at whatever he sets out to do.

John Sylvester Varley (1 April 1956): An English banker and former Group Chief Executive at Barclays Bank. Now a Trustee for the Prince of Wales Charities, he is a trusted intelligent man who knows how best to use money. His traits as an Aries/Monkey makes him a powerful personality.

Miguel Bose (3 April 1956): A Panamanian-born disco/new wave singer, musician and actor. He is a Latin Grammy winner with 7 top ten hits and was a major teen idol in Italy, Spain and Latin America.

Walter Salles (12 April 1956): A Brazilian filmmaker and producer of international prominence. His work revolves around the themes of traveling and search of identity. This Oscar nominated director has been acclaimed as one of the 40 best in the World. He depicts all the best traits of the Aries/Monkey persona.

Alex Da Silva (27 March 1968): A Brazilian champion dancer and choreographer, specializing in salsa dancing. He was also known for being a recurring guest choreographer on the Fox TV show So You Think You Can Dance. In 2012 Da Silva was found guilty of rape and assault with intent to commit rape and was sentenced to ten years in prison. He had defended himself by saying that it had been consensual and that the women were trying to extort money from him. The other side of the Aries/Monkey personality.

David Goodfriend (3 April 1968): An American attorney and advocate in Washington DC. He is a former Administration aide, where he served as Deputy Staff Secretary for President Clinton. He is also the founder and Chairman of Sports Fans Coalition, a coalition of sports activists fighting to give sports fans greater voice in public policy impacting professional and collegiate sports.

Randy Orton (1 April 1980): An American professional wrestler and actor. He is currently signed to WWE. He is a 12 times World Champion, being the youngest to hold the title. He is agile, strong and clever; which entirely fits the description of the Aries/Monkey persona.

CHAPTER 10

ARIES/ROOSTER

THE ARIES/ROOSTER PERSONALITY

This is a happy combination of birth signs, for this merger offers this child a spring of enthusiasm, overflowing with active and positive energy. Now the reason for this positive opening statement is based on the fact that both birth signs are proactive and love to show off, as this self-image increases their self-esteem. For without this external image neither will the Aries be so brave or the Rooster be so up front when they form as one, to show his many abilities. This is because the Aries is the first of our Western Sun Signs and the Rooster is the tenth in the Chinese Personal Twelve Year Cycle. This disparity in their emotional maturity makes the fusion of these impressive characters a challenge for this child, unless supported by the belief that as an individual this Aries/Rooster is doing alright. Because he will have to forge his primitive Aries traits with his more sophisticated Rooster's. However what will weld their differences will be their double need to show off, which will not be too difficult, as this child/youth has enough energy to overcome any problem he finds in his way.

Though at times their different attitudes can be at odds with each other, as the Aries is more immature when matched with the controlled, but still fun-seeking traits of the Rooster. And the reason for this need to balance their disparate traits is due to the shy Rooster's hidden need to be conservative, which is far removed from the Aries impetuosity and disregard for the past. So therefore these birth signs will have to agree to develop a basic form of behaviors, which is both daring, yet well thought out, based on basic logic and backed by traditional values.

Off course this difference isn't the only one to make this merger appear to be all plain sailing, as each sign's negative traits will not merge too well either. Again because of the differences in their maturity, each sign will use different priorities in their thinking patterns, to reach their objectives. Nevertheless, in the majority of cases these extrovert signs will work together to achieve a positive result. Their survival instincts will see to it that any internal problem is solved quickly, in order to portray a person who is seen to be upfront, and who is well able to show off most of his positive traits. Therefore this need will be the energy to make this merger produce a personality who is destined to become a star. Yet it will be up to how this lively Aries/Rooster is nurtured and educated that will decide the future behaviors of this potent personality. Nevertheless, there is more to join these birth signs together than to separate them.

THE POSITIVE TRAITS OF THE ROOSTER:

The Rooster's major positive trait is resilience, for he is able to overcome setbacks, either emotional or practical, because he can be logical in his thinking and can usually self-talk himself into restarting any failed enterprise. This ability leads him to become honest. Simply put, if he believes he is sure of himself he will be able to succeed with even the most difficult projects. This attitude is backed by his enthusiasm to get involved in any activity which will excite him. And to prove he is self-confident, he will have good taste in his dress; at least he will be able to call attention to himself by how good he looks! Plus, and to hide his shyness, he will act with brave and spontaneous frivolity using his simple humor. For his aim is to become popular among his many friends as he needs to feel he is being welcomed in their company, and this image is very much part of his building up his self-esteem.

Plus to add to his image, his inborn traits are mostly based on his logical thinking, which is coolly intellectual, as it helps him to control his wilder emotions. This control alone helps him to develop a strong and steady self-discipline, which strengthens his self-belief, backed with a firmness which leads him to become a rational thinker – particularly during moments of stress. Now most of these diverse traits are not all suited or compatible with those of the fiery Aries. Certainly when his Aries half is being determined and despotic, in wanting to behave in selfish aggressive ways. For this type of basic thinking pattern becomes a challenge when forging and creating a pleasant personality. However this young Rooster's half is lucky to be born with his powerful logical thinking strategies, which will make him become self-centered and so an independent and stoic person who can often overcome many an uncomfortable hurdle, which would floor many other children. And finally this Rooster youth can laugh at himself, at his own silly mistakes, for there is a lot of hidden humor inside his candor. Plus, with his chic dress and behaviors, this union makes his odd and blunt comments acceptable, because he can look a real stunner and be a great comic when he makes his impromptu observations.

THE NEGATIVE TRAITS OF THE ROOSTER:

The Rooster's weaknesses, which are almost unique to this sign, are his cockiness ('Look at me and see how clever I am') which leads him to become loud and verbally abrupt when he thinks he is speaking his truths. Then without a thought to obey common procedures as a leader, he will become too bossy in his methods to control those under his command. Though most of the time he is an able leader, but because he is a strong conservative and mostly traditional, he will tend to become pedantic in the ways he wants things done. He wants to play safe in most of what he does, so as not to feel let down in maintaining his pristine image.

After noting the above weaknesses I can also add the Rooster's loyalty, which can be termed as often foolhardy, due to his support for irrelevant schemes initiated by people he likes or have supported him in the past. In fact he has the tendency to misplace his loyalties, confusing what is honest love with shallow praises, and often with false support, which can lead him to do the work for others to show his loyalty towards them.

These weak traits may seem dire, but this birth sign has a superb survival system to balance these afore mentioned silly traits. Therefore I can state, that rather than this Rooster spending the rest of his life trying to balance his loyalties against his self-protective instincts, he will just use his cool common sense, which will come to his rescue. This will help him decide what's best for him. For after a few let downs, he will become even more of a conservative who will be able to control his bland generosity in the way he offers his support. Particularly when dealing with weak and irrelevant projects. But most importantly his inborn resilience trait, as a good Rooster, will help him come through most let downs. And though his ego will get hurt, his tender naive emotions will not get badly damaged. So he will set off again, in search of his 'El Dorado,' with the added sense of having learned a good lesson.

THE EARLY BEHAVIORS OF THE ARIES/ROOSTER CHILD/YOUTH:

The one good thing in this merger is the positive traits from both of these signs far outweigh his negative ones. At least for most of the time. So generally these two signs do get on together to produce a sensible, sensitive personality. However, the upbringing of this type of child is crucial in order to develop a keen and well-balanced personality. For this Aries/Rooster youth is intelligent and creative, though his actions might well appear otherwise. His parents need to see that from a very young age that he is treated as a responsible person. Providing him with a well-balanced upbringing will achieve maximum benefits. In this way, the fire and excess of the Aries when mixed with the conservative and yet fun seeking extravert traits of the Rooster, will produce a sensible self-controlled child/youth, who can be depended on to behave properly in most occasions.

And I believe this can be done, if his parents are conscious of the potential goodwill inborn in both these birth signs. Because there are so many positive traits, which are very compatible within his makeup, that all they need to do is to love and understand this eager Aries born Rooster to nurture a pleasant personality. Simply because this Aries/Rooster persona is prepared to work hard to achieve his goals. For once he has made up his mind, to fulfill his dreams he will not stop until he has achieved them. Though he might have to go through some inevitable failures first. Particularly during his initial start-up stages, but one thing is certain – he will finally reach his true destiny.

THE ARIES/ROOSTER AS THE FIRST BORN:

At home when young, this Aries/Rooster child will be a bundle of action and good fun, full of true enterprise and humor. Though he would find it difficult to take a no for an answer. He will tend to think he knows it all, with no offense meant, but he will assume that what he wants or needs must be obvious to everyone who loves him. If this Aries/Rooster is born the eldest in his family he would naturally assume the leadership among his siblings. His strong claim to lead would be his honesty and his courage, with which he would speak his mind to keep control of his younger siblings. He will be the same when he speaks his mind with the adults within his family unit.

Not always a sensible diplomatic thing to do, but again this Aries/Rooster thinks that after he has thought things out everyone should agree with him. Though in any family dynamic he will have to learn there are always situations which need careful handling, and not open blunt discussions, where his burning truths are not going to quell family conflicts. Therefore this child/youth will have to learn, mostly the hard way, that it is wiser to hold his tongue until the right moment arrives before offering his solutions to any family misunderstandings. No matter how clear he sees the problem and its solution. Yet I can truly state, in his enthusiasm to help, this honest Aries/Rooster would use a sledge hammer to crack a nut, when a pair of pincers would do.

Returning to this youth's relationships with his siblings, it will be easy to see this Aries/Rooster youth is an able boss who would look after his siblings well enough. A mite too strict at times, but he would mean well in his honest loyal way. His parents therefore would find him a trustworthy and dependable son, always ready to help, his way of course. For once he has made up his mind how to go about doing something, he would stick to his solution, come what may. This stubbornness is very much linked to his self-esteem and personal security. For he has to believe he is sure of what he aims to do before he does it. Thereby only after this intrepid Aries/Rooster has been proven wrong, would he repent and try not to fail again in his duties.

Sad to say this would be the only way most Aries/Rooster youths are going to learn, through their own mistakes. Not because he wants to be stubborn, but because his ego is tied up with his decision making mechanism. He prides himself on having a logical and practical thinking brain, which for most of the time does prove to him he is sensible and balanced in his decision making strategies. This positive self-knowledge gives this Aries/Rooster youth the self-confidence to act the way he does, plus gives him a sense of self-respect and personal values.

THE ARIES/ROOSTER AS THE SECOND CHILD:

If this Aries/Rooster is born in the middle or the youngest in his family, his behavior would be very much the same as above. His resilience to overcome setbacks almost working against him at times. For when he wants something he will go on and on, until he achieves it, without counting the cost to his energy and time, or even getting into trouble, because he will not give up or give in easily. This trait of being headstrong and diligent in not giving up can become a bother for him, and his family, while in others, this stubbornness will certainly help him succeed. For this same tenacity he will use in many of his other ventures, from getting his exams results right, to becoming a sporting champion. However he will still need a lot of sensible guiding and teaching, until as a 'keen and brave Aries/Rooster,' he learns to identify his achievable targets.

THE GENERAL BEHAVIOR OF THE ARIES/ROOSTER:

In any case, this Aries/Rooster will make his personality well known in his household, indeed everywhere he goes. For as an inborn force from very young he will love to be able to show off his many abilities, plus his drive and cockiness. So in order to overcome his enthusiasm, which one could call 'wild behaviors,' he can be happily encouraged to become calmer. And to use his energies to become more helpful and funnier, both at home and at school, indeed anywhere he frequents. Happily he can also be led to become a very useful member of his family during gatherings, by helping with the setting up of all the equipment necessary, to make the party run smoothly. Plus as an extra, he can be allowed to use his entertainment abilities to get everyone involved in the action. This tactic to get this eager Aries/Rooster to be helpful will fulfill several of his needs. For he can be busy in a positive way, plus burn his enthusiasm by getting everyone involved in the fun. And this too will be an excellent opportunity for him to show off his many abilities in a big way.

THE NATURAL BEHAVIORS OF THE ARIES/ROOSTER WITH ADULTS:

In his turn this Aries/Rooster child/youth will cunningly negotiate with his parents or teachers with what he loves to do, in exchange for him keeping a high level of self-control, at home or at school. For example he likes to be dressed smartly, (so the school uniform better be attractive and appealing.) He loves to be admired by the way he is attired because as an Aries/Rooster youth his self-image is very dear to him. I can go as far as to say, that his looks are more important for him than almost any other credit he can wish for. For how he looks is how he will behave, as both these facts are rolled into one image. To give an example, if this Aries/Rooster is dressed as a scruff he will act like one, but if he is dressed smartly, he will act like a Prince. In fact as a personality he could become quite vain and conceited about his neat and clean appearance. For this neat image will make him look after himself and his clothes, so as not to damage his reputation or his clothes. Even his school work will reflect his pride in the status he has at school.

Alongside this need to look smart, this Aries/Rooster will also be careful with his personal hygiene. For part of his self-protection is based on him being clean and fastidious about his cleanliness, and the way his clothes are kept. If not he can be blunt in his views, as he passes judgment on how others should look or behave. To the point he would not have any hesitation to state his honest opinions, which could and do hurt his peers, parents and teachers, if they are not attired properly to suit the occasion. As a traditionalist he believes everyone should be dressed to fit every formal occasion.

He believes this is the best outward sign to show respect, for what the person is about to do, particularly if it is a ceremony in which he is involved. I must remind his fond parents that their Aries/Rooster son is a conservative in his values, for this belief gives him the solid sense of tradition. Which in his eyes means to act smartly is to play safe, as he is backed by his honesty based on what has gone on before, and proven to be correct. For it is easier to come clean in his thinking, than to be sly and devious in his expressions, which he might not be able to keep up at a later date. So, as a personality this Aries/Rooster double birth sign produces a person who finds it easier to be direct, though sometimes blunt, but always honest and loyal.

THE ARIES/ROOSTER AT SCHOOL:

Now to describe what this Aries/Rooster will do at school is a pleasure, because if he has been encouraged by his parents and teachers to do his best, there are no boundaries this brave, eager youth will not attempt to reach. As he will work very hard to show he is a competent student, plus a dependable personality. But it is on the playing fields where he will want to show off the most, as there everyone can see just how good he is as a sportsperson. And to achieve this acclaim status he will practice very hard, even take extra lessons to learn to improve his skills, under a very strict training program. Because it is through his efforts he will demonstrate he is not an empty head, who boasts for the sake of appearing good. Because his boasting is based on his abilities to go beyond the norm, as a true resilient Aries/Rooster.

At the same time I have to admit this Aries/Rooster has a huge weakness, which is his feeling of losing face when he has made a mistake or been told off because of his blunt statements. This fear is highlighted because his double birth signs are very vulnerable to his self-doubts. This fact can be overlooked by his parents and his teachers alike when they try to correct him in front of his peers. Because they can hardly believe that this Aries/Rooster is in fact a shy and sensitive personality, hiding behind his upfront image. For he can normally give the impression he is made out of brass, rather than putty. So in his defense I state, please avoid making this highly sensitive Aries/Rooster youth look foolish when he is trying to do his best. As this situation is a real threat to his self-image and looking incompetent is almost as bad as been seen naked in public.

For as a true Aries/Rooster subject he will deeply believe he has to look good by being smart and acting the correct way. As in effect his self-belief is based on what others think of him, as his image is all tied up with his security blanket. With this I mean, this youth will expect his parents to support him with the same blind faith he supports them with, even when he is not behaving as he should. In fact, his type of self-belief plus his inborn vulnerability can be used as a ready weapon, to get him to keep within his family's or his school's firm boundaries. Of course this type of oblique blackmail should be used sparingly, and only when there is no other way of curbing his bossiness or exuberance.

One support this Aries/Rooster youth does not like, in fact hates, is the constant nagging on the part of any adult near to him, who believes that by pressing him he is going to work any the better. This pressure he believes he does not need. Because he is smart enough to know what is good for him, so there is no need for any pressure to be put on him to perform. This fact his parents and his teachers must know, so they better relax their vigilance, to allow this sensitive intelligent Aries/Rooster youth to mature. Because slowly he will increasingly use his energies to focus on his own school learning, without any need for exterior pressure. For he will have learned from his parents, that having a good level of academic education will be necessary for him to get ahead in his future life, and develop all his inborn potential. As his self-pride alone would see to it he does all he has to do to achieve his best grades with his end of term exams. Which will also provide him with something to boast about. For as a keen and fearless Aries/Rooster student, it would not be proper for his Rooster half not to shine, because his Aries half will put in as much energy as is needed to reach his set targets. As how else will he be able to claim that he is superior!

SUMMARY OF THE ARIES/ROOSTER CHARACTERISTICS AND BEHAVIOR:

☺ Meticulous, foresightedness, confident, charming, cheerful, optimistic, intelligent.

☹ Impetuous, vain, arrogant, selfish, shrewd, cunning, boastful, quick-tempered.

IF THIS CHILD IS MISBEHAVING:

This child is full of positive traits, for he is ambitious and meticulous with clear foresight. He wants to be popular and independent to enjoy his freedom. He is self-confident and mostly helpful, wanting to practice his skills to be able to put his ideas into practice. The other side of him is that he can be annoying; he can become over confident, boastful and a bully. He likes to preach to lead others to where he wants to go. He will try to hide his selfishness by being funny, but really it's to control his environment. In moments of stress, he is either arrogant or aloof trying to hide that he is just shy.

The Aries/Rooster merger produces a formidable personality who needs taming from the start. But do so with reason rather than harshness. At times his actions can either be comical or blunt, which can annoy. The best way to calm him down is to have a quiet but firm word with him at eye level and alone. It is better to harness his energies than abort his good intentions. He loves to show off, use this need to make him work harder at home or school. Then praise him for his efforts. This can then be the way to negotiate with him to keep the peace at home by not trying to dictate what everyone has to do. He will mean well, but he has to start with his own self-discipline. The carrot and the stick is a useful method to adopt. Study his strengths and encourage him self-improve as a way to overcome his weaker moments. Always make him feel important rather than belittle him.

FAMOUS ARIES/ROOSTER PERSONALITIES

Vladimir Peniakoff (30 March 1897): A Belgian-born Russian. He became an officer with the British Armed Forces, commanding a unit of the British Special Forces (nicknamed Popski's Private Army") in the Middle East and Italy during World War II. The role of the unit was reconnaissance, intelligence work and sabotage, for which he was awarded both the Military Cross and the Distinguished Service Order. He was a complex person, given to tearing rages that subsided as quickly as they arose, but with great charm and a wry sense of humor about life's twists and turns. Certainly he can be seen as a true prototype of the Aries/Rooster persona.

Sir Ernst H. Gombrich (30 March 1909): An Austrian/British historian who spent his life in research. He wrote many cultural books, including the Story of Art, which is regarded as one of the most important books on the history of art. He is still considered as the best known art historian in Britain and one of the most influential scholars and thinkers of the 20th century. He was awarded a CBE in 1966, followed by a Knighthood in 1972.

Simone Signoret (25 March 1921): A French cinema actress often hailed as one of France's greatest film stars. In her lifetime she received 2 Césars, 3 BAFTAs, an Emmy, a Cannes Film Festival Award, the Silver Bear for Best Actress award and a Golden Globe nomination.

Peter Ustinov (16 April 1921): An English actor, film producer, screen writer, comedian and UNICEF ambassador. He was awarded a CBE for his services to the film industry. He also won 2 Academy Awards, an Emmy Award, a Golden Globe plus a BAFTA Award.

Claude Cohen-Tannoudji (1 April 1933): A French physicist. He shared the 1997 Nobel Prize in Physics with 2 other scientists for research in methods of laser cooling and trapping atoms. He was still an active researcher working at the Ecole Normale Supérieure in Paris in 2018.

Roy Clark (15 April 1933): An American country music musician and performer. He is best known for hosting the "Hee-Haw," a national television Country Variety Show from 1969 to 1992. He is still active in his 80s! He has been a member of the Grand Ole Opry since 1987, and is inducted in the Country Music Hall of Fame.

Montserrat Caballé (19 April 1933): A world-renowned Spanish operatic soprano singer. She has sung a wide variety of roles, but she is best known as an exponent of the works of Verdi, Rossini, Bellini, and Donizetti. She came to the attention of a much wider audience when she recorded 'Barcelona', a duet with Freddie Mercury, the lead singer of the British rock band Queen for the 1992 Olympic Games. In 2015 she was found guilty of tax evasion and handed a six-month suspended jail sentence. She did not go as she paid her dues, and her reputation also helped.

Eric Clapton (30 March 1945): An English rock singer, song-writer and guitarist. He is the only three-time inductee to the Rock and Roll Hall of Fame: once as a solo artist and separately as a member of the Yardbirds and of Cream. He has been referred to as one of the most important and influential guitarists of all time. He has also won 18 Grammy Awards, a CBE for his services to music, plus many more accolades.

Lee Jong-Wook (12 April 1945): A Korean doctor. He was the Director General of the World Health Organization for three years between 2003 and 2006. He studied both in Seoul and Hawaii Universities to achieve his degrees in Health Care. He was highly regarded as a world leader in health care, working to improve the health of millions of people, from combating tuberculosis and HIV/AIDS to his aggressive efforts to eradicate polio. In 2004 Time magazine named him as one of the world's one hundred most influential people.

Michael Lehmann (30 March 1957): An American film and television director. Through hard work and study he slowly worked his way up the ladder to become a recognized top director. He has been awarded many accolades for his work in films and TV shows. One can hardly expect less from a successful active Aries/Rooster.

Seve Ballesteros (9 April 1957): A Spanish world-renowned golfer. He played a leading role in European golf, helping the European Ryder Cup team to five wins both as a player and captain. He has become an icon in the sport having won more than 90 international tournaments in his career, including the Open Championship three times, and the Masters Tournament twice. He is hailed as one of the most talented and exciting golfers to ever play the game. Now his son has become a professional golf player himself.

Mikhail Pletnev (14 April 1957): A Russian concert pianist, composer and conductor. He entered the Soviet Music School at 13 and by age 21 he had won a Gold Medal and First Prize at the Moscow Tchaikovsky Competition, which earned him international recognition and attention worldwide. He founded the Russian National Orchestra in 1990, with the help of Mikhail Gorbachev, the then Leader of the Soviet Union.

Mariah Carey (27 March 1969): An American singer, songwriter and actress. Referred to as the 'Songbird Supreme' by the Guinness World Records. She became famous after releasing her self-titled debut studio album which was a great success. She has won 5 Grammy Awards, 19 World Music Awards, 10 American Music Awards and 14 Billboard Music Awards, and has been consistently credited with inspiring a generation of singers. She is now Columbia Record's top selling artist, making more money than most other artists.

Mellody Hobson (3 April 1969): An American businesswoman and president of Ariel Investments, and the former Chair of the Board of Directors of DreamWorks Animation. In 2017 she became the first African-American woman to head The Economic Club of Chicago and in 2018 she was named as Vice-Chair of Starbucks Corporation. Her work ethic and charm have helped her to be promoted above many other applicants. A true Aries/Rooster personality, full of enthusiasm, plus hard work, with the show-of-power to achieve her targets.

CHAPTER 11

ARIES/DOG

THE ARIES/DOG PERSONALITY

The combination of the Aries and the Dog year is not an easy combination to merge, because this child can be too honest and bold for his own good. It could appear, that he is a reborn Crusader, whose intention and mission in life are to put right what he believes is wrong. Plus urge his family and near friends to become perfect. And I am not exaggerating, for these united birth signs traits are forceful and honest, with the simple intention to do good. For the Aries offers his views projecting his simple needs, in a straightforward way, demonstrated by his basic skills in any action he is involved in.

And the Dog's needs are to feel he is being protected by his family, and at the same time he will try to protect others. The one mitigating aspect of this combination is, that though the Aries sign is the first in our Western Zodiac, with its basic needs geared to pleasing himself, the Dog is second to last, in the Chinese Personality Cycle, which has a maturity, which will tame most of the Aries rash judgments and single-minded actions.

In fact this combination will create a very hard-working, and dynamic personality, when it comes to being a vigilant caretaker. Though at times this Aries/Dog will demonstrate his selfish-powers and at other times his determination to help others, beyond the call of duty. Even when he has not been asked! But one thing is certain, this double birth sign makes for a strong personality, because most of his inborn traits are strong. And the best note to describe this combination is, that the welding of their separate survival instincts will see to it, that the balance in the merging of their negative traits, conforms to the expected behaviors, in order to produce a pleasant and hardworking personality.

THE POSITIVE TRAITS OF THE DOG:

The Dog is full of constancy, meaning that no matter what he is asked to do, he will do it as best he can, to please his parents. For this is the way he shows his love, for those who love and protect him, and this obedience is the way he returns these affections with his stoic respectability. For almost like a pedigree Dog, he will always want to appear sensible and trustworthy to his kind. He is also lucky to have a logical left brain intelligence, which helps him with the way he carries out his duties, as he puts into practice, what he thinks has to be put right. And to prove his Dog's loyalty and true inborn characteristics, he believes that he is born to protect his family. In the first place, then the world at large. And to do this he will be able to become full of heroism, with self-disregard in any number of dangerous situations.

THE NEGATIVE TRAITS OF THE DOG:

A Dog's weakness is that of his personal uneasiness, because he is constantly on the look-out for trouble. By this I mean that everything around him has to fit in within his security/strategy, as he will expect his parents to be as loyal to him as he is towards them. And if and when he perceives that something is wrong in his opinion, he will be ready to criticize the person or the event he does not agree with. This self-righteous opinion can lead him to become tactless, as he points out the errors he sees in his immediate environment. In short this Dog individual can become a pain within his family's easy-going attitude. Because he sees his needs with a view, that everything around him has to be right and safe. So that he knows he is secure in his surroundings. As with this feeling of safety, he will buttress his personal security. Yet one can hardly blame him for behaving as a Dog, for his vigilance is very much part of his survival instincts, which lead him to become extra careful, but very dependable.

But as a mitigating statement I also have to add, it is most important for this Dog being throughout his life to be able to feel safe. So that he feels he is being protected from the known or even unknown perils. For having this security will make him become a very reliable, stoic personality, who will do what he has to do, to help himself and others, without any self-doubting. The other side of this self-assurance is, that as this child grows older, he can become more than a little cynical when he sees what he thinks is carelessness in other people, who are not as cautious as he. This evidence will give him the belief, that he is superior to those people who are not as fully aware as he. This truth can now explain why at times this Aries/Dog youth can become a little haughty in his dealings with others. Because his feeling of being superior is very much tied up with his own security blanket, and self-esteem, which allows him to be blunt and forthright.

THE WELDING OF THE ARIES AND DOG CHARACTERISTICS:

Hence the sum total of this combination of traits gives this child/youth a good foundation to build on, regarding his manners and again his high moral values. Though all these fastidious Dog traits can become a little difficult-to-put-up-with, when added to those of the primitive, strong and basic traits of the Aries. But happily the Dog's traits can also (at times) become an aid to help the Aries to see beyond his narrow thinking patterns, to realize that he is not the only one with needs. I have to add here, that the Chinese Astrologers choose this Dog's character descriptions very well, to express the characteristics inborn in its human counterpart both in his positive, as well as in his negative behaviors.

THE REASONS FOR THE ARIES/DOG'S NEED TO FEEL SUPERIOR:

Being superior is this child/youth's answer when he feels he is being threatened by someone who he believes is acting as superior as he does! He believes that using this ploy of being cynical is his best way to defend himself when he is faced with a good chance of being discovered. He can be full of self-doubts about himself, and not too sure of his intended image, so to hide this vulnerability the Dog will use any strategy to make himself be seen as important, so he is judged as a serious and trustworthy personality, particularly by all those adults who have to deal with him in his day to day life routines and behaviors. It is very important to him that he portrays the image that he is being sensible, dependable and honest in the way he behaves with his peers, both at school and at home. His main claim to all these positive adjectives is his need to display his heroic deeds, and that his noble unselfish actions overshadow any of his self-known weaknesses, which he prefers to keep hidden.

THE EARLY BEHAVIORS OF THIS ARIES/DOG CHILD/YOUTH:

The one good thing about this merger is that when these disparate traits of the Aries/Dog do merge, the positive elements of each sign seem to flower, and the result is the birth of a talented, dutiful, and even a heroic child. Though at the same time a child who has very strong views on honesty, and who will be very quick to point out any underhand dealings or inconsistency in all areas of his understanding.

Yet this trait of wanting to be honest, in what he sees as justice, almost forces him to become far too ridged in his views. Especially as he will make judgmental comments about what is actually happening around him. These comments will make his points of view sound as an immature avenger, who is ready and able to point a finger at any person or situation he does not agree with. And he will base his condemnation on his assessment that he suspects the person he's criticizing is not being honest with his truths. Now this might well be correct, for this child/youth has a highly-tuned sense of detection, based on his survival instincts, which work like a radar.

Now it is important to bear in mind that this young Aries/Dog's observations are interpretations of his immature reasoning based on his basic limited range of personal truths. So being annoyed with him because of his big mouth can be mitigated and almost forgiven, because of his need to be seen as honest. As being truthful helps him feel he is worthy of being protected by his parents when he needs it. So I plea for his forgiveness, as he only wants to be loved, respected and protected by being seen as a dependable personality. Though he has to be warned to keep a tight control over his blunt tongue, as he can cause more trouble than he can imagine when he is speaking his truths.

THE CHANGE IN THIS ARIES/DOG AS HE MATURES:

If this Aries/Dog youth was to become conscious of the trouble he can cause when he speaks his truths, he would keep his mouth shut. But here is the rub, any unfairness seen by this child will be perceived as a threat to his own security. So that he can feel safe in his environment he depends on everything being practical and fair and most of his awkward comments are meant to point out where his safety limits are within which he will feel protected. However, to make a positive comment, as this Aries/Dog child/youth matures his view of his limitations will expand, until he can control most of his own life and his fears will diminish. So the best way to deal with this Aries/Dog's early vulnerability is to get him to understand that life in general is not seen as being fair by most unsatisfied people, because they are looking after themselves first, just as he does!

REASONING WITH THE ARIES/DOG:

This type of explanation, might take some time for this child to understand, but it is better to try than get irritated with his daily pouring of negative comments, as he judges what other people are doing. The lesson here is he has to learn to accept, that he is not always right, and neither are most other people wrong. It just means they have different interests and opinions on the same matter to his own priorities. On reading this explanation it could appear farfetched to this vigilant Aries/Dog youth, and sound far too deep an explanation to give this young personality. Though I believe this sensitive child will slowly understand, that people do have different opinions on the same matter. Though he will think that his opinion is the best one!

THE ARIES/DOG AS THE FIRST BORN IN THE FAMILY:

If this Aries/Dog is born the eldest in his family he would want his siblings to obey him, without any questions. For he would believe that obedience to his family's rules and habits is his evidence to show his love and protection towards his siblings. For certainly he would try to love and protect them from all dangers, real or imaginary, and this close attention will satisfy his own needs. His siblings in turn would find him a bit of a dictator, with a kind heart and who is always ready to help them. Though he is a stickler for keeping the house rules. For this Aries/Dog's aim is to give his charges the same love and protection he himself would love to receive from his parents. And though his love could become more than a bit claustrophobic, his siblings would feel safe within his company, and accept it as part of his love for them. Because instinctively they would know he means the best for them, in the only way he knows how.

THE ARIES/DOG AS THE SECOND CHILD:

If this Aries/Dog is born in the middle or the youngest in his family he would try very hard to have his voice heard, and his plans carried out, as soon as he is able to speak up. For he would state quite clearly that his game plans are the best, because he has thought about them before hand, and they would be safer than any other idea. Simply because he is part Aries there is this irresistible need for him to lead. So it will be easy for him to believe he has the right to do so, albeit by being dogmatic and persistent with his views. For his views of life are that everything is either black or white, and he is able to decide what is which because of his passion for the truth. By this I mean that before he speaks out about what he wants to do, he will have thought about it diligently, to make sure that his plans are both safe and fun. But most of all his plans will make sure that he is the leader and everyone else is under his control. And to prove his sincerity in all his intentions he would state heroically, that he would 'die' for his family, to make sure all were safe under his care. Happily, as this intrepid Aries/Dog child matures, he will learn to listen to other people's opinions before he demands his plans are 'fool-proof.' Though he would only listen to what others have to say so that he can to find holes in their plans.

THE GENERAL MATURITY OF THE ARIES/DOG:

However the most charming characteristic of this Aries/Dog's youth is in his main endeavor to achieve a perfect world, at home and at school. For this state of perfection would provide him with the happy satisfaction that he is being useful. And this thought would make him feel more positive about himself, plus help him enhance his self-confidence, which in turn would encourage him to develop many of his other natural talents. For instinctively he will enjoy helping, which will make him feel safer in the company of those who admire him, after he has helped them.

But if those who he has just helped do not openly admire him, he would get into a state of disbelief even depression. Because he would believe all his good work would have come to naught. Meaning that he had wasted his time and energies on ratters, who do not appreciate his good intentions. Not what he had envisaged in the first place as he set out to promote himself. Now, if this sad event were to happen, the best way to lift up his down cast spirits is to remind him of his past successes. Certainly this type of encouragement would make him to feel much better in himself and to quickly forget his frustrations. For happily his Aries half would react positively after listening to those positive words from his parents. Because, as a true Aries/Dog, he will still want to continue feeling good about himself, plus he can continue showing off, which is very much part of his mental makeup.

THE NEED FOR THE ARIES/DOG TO HAVE A GOOD TIME:

Up to now I have been a little serious in describing this Aries/Dog's weaker traits. But I am sure if his parents encouraged him to join them for a bit of family fun, these efforts would improve his life style, and lighten-up his otherwise dull image. So I recommend that both his parents and his teachers should set out to encourage this potential Saint to become more spontaneous in his actions. In fact to appeal to his Aries side, so that he does enjoy taking some adventurous risks by involving himself with others, without having the need to lead or protect them. And most of all he should look after himself by having more fun time, and not to become so serious about what others are doing, over which he has no control. For the end result in living his life has to be to become more positive about himself, which would help him build a new image, with the idea of helping himself first before setting out to help others. With this new attitude he would have to rethink how best to help others, if there is a need. For there is nothing wrong in wanting to enjoy himself, by being a little selfish, regardless of what others want him to do for them. This new image would mean he will have to concentrate on his own needs and not what he expects he needs to do for others. Not easy for the mental makeup of an Aries/Dog.

RECOMMENDED ACTIVITIES TO HELP
THE ARIES/DOG:

One idea to help this Aries/Dog to concentrate on himself is to get him to join an adventure sports club so that he can enjoy organized activities, which would appeal to his Aries half. And at the same time he will be able to learn what to do for his own self-protection (like the skills needed in all types of rescues) which is something that would please his Dog half. Then, as he is also half Aries, the thrill of overcoming his fears by rafting down a swift river will help him to feel good within himself. Surviving a good soaking among others who are just as eager to enjoy the action, but without him having to supervise the activity, will make him realize that he has to live his life through his own experiences, and during these moments of action he can test himself and see how others admire him for his bravery!

But I have to repeat that to keep this Aries/Dog youth happy he has to feel he will be protected in whatever he does. So after this safety element has been settled, he will then happily join any game or activity, without having to be pushed into it. In fact I believe the best way to get him motivated, and away from feeling the fear of being vulnerable, is for him to dedicate his time to study at school and beyond. As the knowledge gained through this wider study will get him to understand the importance for him to self-test himself through his own efforts. And his academic successes will help him to overcome his natural fears, even if he does fail at first because of his self-doubts. But by motivating his Aries half he can always try again. Because failing is not a weakness, but a sign he has to try harder for improve himself.

THE BEST WAY TO HELP THE ARIES/DOG CHILD TO
OVERCOME HIS FEARS:

This has to be done as soon as this child/youth shows any hesitation in trying to avoid doing anything he is not sure about. For he has to be told that feeling fear is a natural feeling, which most human beings have as it is part of our survival instincts. He can overcome this feeling by practicing his self-belief that he can survive, as this bravery is also part of our mental makeup, providing we take the necessary precautions to avoid getting hurt. But in his case, he is lucky being born an Aries, for he can overcome his self-doubts by his sheer bravery. And as a Dog he can plan to protect himself first, before attempting something new. So this is how he has to see his life, using both his birth signs. One to take a risk, and the other to be able to foresee any danger before it happens. This indeed reads as brainwashing, and it is. But this Aries/Dog child needs this type of emotional blackmail to surmount his Dog's fears of failure, so as not to look bad within his family circle, for how else can he be seen as the protector?

SUMMARY OF THE ARIES/DOG CHARACTERISTICS AND BEHAVIOR:

☺ Respectful, sincere, loyal, quick-witted, honest, helpful, kind-hearted.

☹ Anxious, restless, worried, dogmatic, serious, impatient, defensive.

IF THIS CHILD IS MISBEHAVING:

This child is quick-witted, honest and wants to be as helpful as possible. Within a strict family he will be ready to obey, but in a loose family he will want to rule. He can be demanding and of others with a cool head, wanting peace and safety at home and order at school. He loves to be active helping his parents, but insisting he has better ideas than most. He does this to become popular as this makes him feel needed and safe. He doesn't tolerate inactivity well so will have little patience with people who are slower. He hates being misunderstood, but he is also blunt in the way he expresses himself, causing family upset when all he wants is to bring order among his peers. He is a conservative who wants to play safe and wants to stop others from making mistakes. In wanting to make his world better so that he can be safe and be able to help those he considers victims, he will preach his thoughts and concerns with enthusiasm.

The merger of these different birth signs is not easy. Therefore his behaviors will swing from being selfish to wanting to help. The best way to tame this youth is to have him follow a set plan of action, almost like a trained dog. So being firm with him will not upset him as he depends on law and order to feel safe. Listen to him but do not argue, but allow him to help by following strict rules. Certainly use his energies in a positive way by helping at home and receiving good reports from school. He likes being responsible, so put him in charge of an activity. Allow him to protest and agree when necessary, then reward his efficient methods with a kind word. Remember, he is an active dog, so he will prefer to be patted on the head rather than made to look a fool. His temper has to be controlled, but not with force but through isolation.

FAMOUS ARIES/DOG PERSONALITIES

Gustave Moreau (6 April 1826): A French symbolic painter and writer, whose main interest was to illustrate scenes of the bible and mythological figures. He had a big influence over other artists through the bold way he expressed his style of paintings. He was known for his eccentricity and his prolific output, as he produced over 8,000 works of art during his lifetime.

Harry Houdini (24 March 1874): An American escapologist. He was a world renowned stunt man, magician and entertainer, who hated the false miracle makers. So he spent much of his life uncovering tricksters, though he himself was endowed with psychic powers, which he used to form his own tricks. A pity he died young, pretending his was invincible.

Ludwig Mies Van der Roke (27 March 1886): An American/German designer, renowned for his modern furniture designs and architectural projects. He is regarded as a pioneer of Modern Architecture. He wanted to show his ideas on how to design buildings, which had extreme clarity, simplicity and efficiency. He was awarded the President's Medal for Freedom in 1963. A true prototype for the Aries/Dog personality.

Erich Gimpel (25 March 1910): A German spy who managed to enter the USA to spy on the activities of the America Army. He was a difficult man to catch red-handed, but when he was finally caught he resisted interrogation. So he was sent to prison, rather than 'opening his mouth' to give details of his mission, demonstrating his Dog's loyal personality.

Karl Albrecht (28 March 1922): A German entrepreneur who founded the discount supermarket chain Aldi with his brother Theo. He started from a small corner shop in war-torn Germany. By working hard and by being inventive, he and his brother are now considered to be amongst the richest men in Germany.

Doris Day (3 April 1922): An American stage and film star, singer and dancer. She had her own TV show for many years. She recorded more than 650 songs and appeared in over 39 films. She was ranked as the biggest box office star for 4 years from 1960/64. For this she was rewarded with many prestigious awards from the Hollywood film industry.

Julius Nyerere (13 April 1922): The president of Tanzania from 1964 to 1985. He worked very hard to bring peace and freedom to Africa. He was a great scholar, philosopher and a tireless keen political worker. He represents the very essence of the Aries/Dog personality.

Carlo Rubbia (31 March 1934): An Italian particle physicist. In 1984 he jointly shared with Simon van der Meer the Nobel Prize in Physics for the discovery of the massive, short-lived subatomic W particle and Z particle. His work enabled the formulation of new methods for studying particle collisions and asteroid 8398 Rubbia is named in his honor. In 2013 he was appointed to the Senate of Italy as a Senator for Life.

Jane Goodall (3 April 1934): An English primatologist and anthropologist, she is considered the world's foremost expert on chimpanzees. She has received many honors for her environmental and humanitarian work, including being named a UN Messenger of Peace in 2002 and created a Dame of the British Empire in 2003.

Colette Besson (7 April 1946): A French athlete, winner of the Gold medal for the 400 meters at the 1968 Mexico Olympics. She surprised the world of sport and became a French national heroin. During her career she set up many records for the 4-by-400 meters, as the anchor member of the French relay team.

Marsha A. Hunt (15 April 1946): An American singer, song writer, novelist and actress. She was involved with Mick Jagger for a time (a demanding character.) Neither did she have an easy life after leaving him, for she had to fight cancer and other calamities. But she kept up her spirits, becoming a proactive personality and an example for many other sufferers.

Cazuiza (4 April 1958): A Brazilian poet, composer and a top exponent of Brazilian Rock Music. He helped to make his type of music popular at home and world-wide. He has sold over 5 million albums, plus achieving 11 number one singles in a 9 year period. His life story is the prototype of the Aries/Dog personality.

Nigel Slater (9 April 1958): An English cook who is well known as a TV chef, food writer, journalist and broadcaster. He has helped to make cooking popular among the millions who watch his shows. Plus he has also taught how to cook a balanced meal for nutritional, as well as for its looks and tastes.

Kevin M. Warsh (13 April 1970): An American lawyer and economist. He was involved as a Government official and prominent figure in the Reserves for the USA monetary system. He is a member of both the Group of Thirty and the Steering Committee of the Bilderberg Group. A smart Aries/Dog, who loves to work hard and shares his knowledge with all those around him.

CHAPTER 12

ARIES/PIG

THE ARIES/PIG PERSONALITY

This is a good combination for these two astrological birth signs; the Aries and the Pig Year. For if this child is brought up in a balanced environment, this merger of signs will result in a very positive union as this child will tend to become a very lively, intelligent and loving member of his family. I state, in a balanced family, because both these birth signs are naturally strong personalities, so this child's nurturing has to be planned to be homely, but strict, for any weakness shown during his upbringing will make this Aries/Pig take over the running of his household. This child's main interest will be to get what he wants, plus to feel he has complete self-protection alongside his family and friends. Yet, at the same time he is being looked after, he will expect that most of his natural talents are being recognized and developed because his parents care for him.

Consequently, from a very young age, this Aries/Pig should behave very well indeed, causing no troubles at home, but making sure he is not denied any of his wishes. For he would judge his parents love towards him according to how he receives their love and his many material wishes. This selfish attitude is all due to his natural insecurities, which makes him feel vulnerable when he is not in control of his environment. As an

Aries, he is basically a primitive thinker in his needs, but as a Pig he is very mature in the ways he wants to be looked after.

So outwardly, when this Aries/Pig is feeling unsafe he will behave in a peaceful manner, even though inwardly he would be torn apart by his conflicting emotions because he wants to be protected by having all his wishes granted to the point of being excessive, just as any Arian. Then, if he does not receive what he wants, he will get into a raging temper. This time because he is a Pig, and this is the way he reacts when he feels cheated. Happily, these temper tantrums only happen when he is being provoked and he feels defenseless because he is not achieving what he believes is his right. But normally this Aries/Pig will behave very well indeed, particularly when he is outside his home, for his aim is to portray the image that he has a pleasant personality. As in this way he will be able to demand his due for his good behaviors. This is especially true when he is finding it difficult to get what he wants from his parents or friends. Therefore, there is an underlying feeling that this child has the potential to become aggressive when he is frustrated. But he is smart enough to cover this vibration with a coating of smooth talk. He can also become very funny to displace any tension.

THE POSITIVE TRAITS OF THE PIG:

There are many positive traits found in the Pig which are; his intellectual honesty, leading him to become a gallant personality. This helps him become full of sincerity as he looks around himself to collect as much information as possible from those near to him. Later, with this acquired knowledge, he will use what he considers useful for him as a base for his own truths. All this study then allows him to show an in-depth knowledge of different behaviors, even cultures. Finally to prove that he is born to be 'superior,' he will act with tact and common sense, for he needs to feel above others in support of his social awareness to show he is an example for clean, honest living.

All this show of pleasantness is to safeguard his security blanket, which for him means that he is being fully backed by his parents, because he tries to show loyalty towards them as well as to behave correctly. He will be well aware of his need for his parent's support because despite all of his show of superiority, he still has his self-doubts like, 'Am I good-enough?' So he will need the love of his parents to buttress his lack of personal credibility when he is still young, simply because he is so mature in his thinking that he is aware of his lack of experience. So to override his fears he will behave the best he can in and out of the home. Needless to say, all these Pig's traits are much more refined than those of the fiery Aries, for they involve a deeper sense of self-awareness and a higher sense of civilized behaviors.

As an aside, I have to state that the Pig's personality is regarded as having the combined character traces of all the other eleven year signs preceding it. The reason for this assumption is that the wise Chinese Astrologers came to the conclusion that, with each year that passed, the personality they were describing became more self-aware and mature. And as this Pig year is the last of their 12 year personality cycle, they then assumed that it would have the sum total of experiences from all the other previous signs. I do believe that this year sign does have traces of many of the other year signs, but mostly when this Pig is acting in an extreme way, and his behaviors are not always the appropriate ones. Happily though, these odd behaviors are not often seen during this child's day to day life, even though he will react when he is provoked by being overlooked or cheated. In short, this Pig year is not to be seen as an ordinary year, as it seems to have an uncanny depth of maturity, as well as a naivety which can be seen as a first-year sign. In effect, this year sign can produce a very wise and charming personality who can be very naïve as well as helpful, but certainly more ambitious than many other years.

THE NEGATIVE TRAITS OF THE PIG:

The Pig's weaknesses are his momentary hesitations before he sets about doing any activity when he is with other children. This delay is due to his self-doubts about deciding what his best tactics are to gain the maximum leadership powers with the least amount of energy. At the same time, he does not want to show that he feels vulnerable because of his self-doubts. So to cover up for his obvious hesitation, he will pretend he is busy in order to hide the fact that he is using his skills for simple manipulations. This means he will wait till he is ready to act, without creating a fuss, while pretending to be minding his own business. And the one way he can disguise his delay is to share his many toys with his peers.

This alone will build up his reputation for being friendly and popular because of his generosity. But to fulfil this strategy, he will want more toys than most of his friends. Toys he will demand from his parents as his needs, or his birth right! But if he does not get what he wants, or fails in his tactics to convince his parents to buy him more, he will get angry and then either sulk or cry in a temper. But worse still, if he feels as an honest Aries/Pig that his well-planned intentions are being abused or misunderstood by his brothers or friends, he will get into a rage. But as a safeguard against showing his few weaknesses, which he is well aware of, he will become stubborn, standoffish and even pig-headed to avoid his tantrums.

GENERAL NOTES ON THE ARIES/PIG PERSONALITY:

However, I feel I have to explain the reasons for this Aries/Pig's extreme behaviors. They are all tied up with his sense of self-protection, as part of enhancing his security blanket, for he needs to feel noticed and respected as a forerunner for his inventive ideas and his smart creativity. This forged self-vision then leads this Aries/Pig to feel important, for he knows that most important people are normally well protected. This attitude for wanting to become important can induce him to take on any difficult challenge which is presented to him, no matter how stressful. This, in fact, is a good trait to have and to develop, as well as his natural ability to show his understanding and down to earth problem solving attitudes, which he shows towards his family and friends simply because he can detach from their immature emotional thinking patterns, even as a young person, to solve mundane childish problems.

For his main personal interest is to love and protect himself first, so he can well afford to become detached, even from the people he most loves. This coolness therefore helps him see through the selfish behaviors in others in stark reality. Though when his self-interests are at play he will act very differently, for he will feel vulnerable or unloved if he stands outside his family's orbit. Then this Aries/Pig will start looking for something to eat to calm his anxieties. Now this habit can bring on more problems than it can solve. Because to have a stomach full of rubbish food just because it tastes good does not help his mental state in the long run. Not to mention the damage it will cause his health if he becomes overweight at a young age. It is therefore important for the parents of this Aries/Pig to be aware that his taste buds are a bad councilor for healthy eating. The suggestion has to be to enjoy physical exercises instead of overeating to solve anxiety problems. So getting fit and partaking in friendly competitions is the best way to control any emotional stresses. Now this weakness does not attack all Aries/Pigs youths, but a good number can suffer from this need to appease their fear of failure by stretching their stomach pouches.

But in general, the Aries/Pig is a happy mixture of traits which can produce a child who is comfortable in what he believes in and in what he is wants to know. This trait of being able to discern through self-gained knowledge will wisely help him discover what is best for him. Plus, when this ability is added to his keen dynamic ambitions, the result is the forming of a powerful personality who needs to be seen as an important and, therefore powerful personality, at least within his family and with most friends. Certainly to earn this image is important for an Aries/Pig's self-confidence, even from a young age, though he will try to hide his love for material goods knowing that it causes him to be envied.

Yet he is prepared to face this challenging hurdle as he will still feel his possessions enhance his prestige value. However, to lessen his obvious greed he will try to be generous, as he will give away the objects he no longer needs in the hope that he is going to receive back some sort of quick reward from those he has been kind with.

THE ARIES/PIG'S BEHAVIOR AT HOME WHEN YOUNG:

An Aries/Pig child will be quick to show promise in his involvement within his family structure, and later on at school, for he will or should show that he is quick in his learning and is interested in most topics presented to him. Plus, he will show a willingness to participate in most activities taking place around him, as an Aries/Pig loves to compete in order to prove himself and his capabilities in all areas of his young life. And he is brave enough to try to fit into any of the many challenges he will meet during his everyday life. Instinctively, his aim will be to perfect his personal development by trying to self-test himself continuously, as he knows that he can feel vulnerable and inadequate in new situations. Unfortunately, sometimes during these self-testing times he may think he is being misunderstood, or he may believe that his good intentions to learn new skills are being ridiculed. Then he will fly into a temper, for he dislikes being made fun off when he is trying to improve himself.

Though the real reason for this explosion is hidden, even from this young Aries/Pig's thinking process, because at first he will feel the anger of being embarrassed, at being seen to look silly. Then he will feel his shame, because he will fear that he is showing his vulnerability. And lastly he will know that he should be smart enough to overcome any difficulty with which he is faced. So the combined result of all these self-doubts is that he will get into an unwanted rage. The best way to deal with him is to sit him apart, give him something to drink or eat, and just left alone to calm himself, which he will.

He will not need any further help to self-control his state of anger, for all he needs to know is the understanding and reassurance from his parents, who love and support him even though his actions during the time he is angry are not always acceptable. However, when he does calm down, it has to be pointed out to him that there is no need for him to lose his temper when he feels angry, because not only does he give a poor impression of himself, but to regain his lost image will take him time and effort. These sensible words will calm him down even further and teach him that, if he wants to look important or superior, he will have to control his emotions. Happily, sooner rather later, this Aries/Pig will eventually manage to restrain his quick temper by using his cooler positive traits, which he knows are naturally mature and will give him a better image.

THE ARIES/PIG AS THE FIRST BORN:

If this Aries/Pig is born the eldest in his family he would love to rule his siblings. For becoming a leader is very much part of his inborn needs, as he requires to show his cool prowess, his bravery and his natural intelligence, as well as his ability to look after himself and others. So, in his desire to show his love for his siblings, he would become too protective and controlling, to the point that he might well overdo it. So as a result of this excess protection, it could well lead him to being rejected by his siblings. Now this would really make him feel betrayed, but for his own good this would be a necessary lesson for him to learn. As he has to learn that he cannot own the people he loves. I believe this young person will need lots of good and clear explanations from his parents to teach him, and that to show his love towards his brothers and sisters does not mean he has to 'live their life.' And certainly, explain to him that he should avoid showing any excess in his controlling tactics, which will make his siblings reject him even though he means well.

THE ARIES/PIG AS THE SECOND CHILD:

However, if this Aries/Pig is born in the middle or is the youngest in his family, he would like to do his own thing as soon as he is able, regardless of what his older siblings want to do. The simple reason for this attitude is that his sense of individuality is again tied up with his security blanket and his sense of superiority, for he will prefer to have people he trusts guide him, not other children who he feels are below his practical abilities. This sense of superiority is tied up with his maturity, which can at time be more developed than other children's. Therefore, he would normally find it difficult to follow other children's plans unless he has had an important input into the proposed action. And to make things even more difficult for him, as a member of any group, he has an inborn trait to meddle with what is going on around him. For he would tend to think that his ideas are better than those of others because of his highly developed self-preservation thinking patterns.

THE ARIES/PIG AT SCHOOL:

This type of mature thinking would show up at school where an Aries/ Pig would be self-motivated to study hard and so gain top marks. For he will soon discover that those children who try to do well receive certain privileges as an incentive to continue with their attentive learning. This quick discovery alone would motivate him to be at the top end of his class list, firstly for his own good and the good of others, and he would want his parents to be proud of him. What might come as a surprise, even to him, is his positive inborn traits for becoming naturally artistic in a creative sort of way. So once this talent has come to light, he should be motivated and taught to practice any of his many creative talents from drawing, to mixing colors, to painting, even to learning to play a musical instrument, etc.

Then, as an Arian, he would also like to be on the stage, on show. In fact, an Aries/Pig will do anything to be seen in the limelight. Therefore, this keen interest in acting should be encouraged, if and when it appears for it will teach him to follow strict orders from the stage director. He would benefit from this discipline as it would teach him to become funnier, rather than angrier, when he gets frustrated, particularly when he is not chosen to become the main actor of any show because he is too ambitious. So he will soon learn that behaving like the angry young man will not help him get the main roles, no matter how hard he tries. This truth alone will make him realize that he better calm down and behave himself.

THE ARIES/PIG IN HIS TEENAGE YEARS:

But to return to the dilemma inborn within the Aries/Pig personality; as he matures, due to his constant identity battle, he will feel like he is walking on a tight rope. For on one side he wants to appear superior, as the adventurous Aries, while on the other side as the Pig he feels hesitant and indecisive, because he does not want to look foolish. No wonder he can become a great actor, playing the funny role in any comedy, and then the tragic role in a drama. For in his daily life experiences these emotions will teach him which role to play to keep his head just above water. But on the positive side, his demanding ego will in fact aid him in his learning, for he will comply with what he is told to do whether he likes it or not, just to progress in his learning and so prove himself to be a good student. He will always want to do well, to save face. But the rub is, if he thinks he has been given a free choice as to what subjects to study, he will comply with the advice he receives from his parents or his favorite teachers. However if this Aries/Pig believes he is being bullied or harassed by his parents or teachers to do work he does not agree with, he will then rebel, feeling that he is being oppressed and that his free will has being tempered with.

Happily this young Aries/Pig spark will normally behave well, being full of positive and honest intentions. For he knows full well that it is better for him to portray that he is full of fun and positive determination than be negative, which inevitably will get him into trouble. Generally, his main attitude towards his studies will always be to do the right thing. For himself first, and then for others, as being true to his inborn traits he wants to be seen as an honest and honorable student so that others may see him as the 'Knight in white armor.' This ideal would be very much part of his persona, because through being seen as mature he will become more conservative as he grows older. At least he can pretend to be more serious, and this will give his self-image the role of the reliable student. The one thing I strongly recommend to help this Aries/Pig is that he should be motivated to continue with his extra academic studies, if he shows the capacity to do so. Because, as a true Aries/Pig, he has enough personal ambition to face the hard slog of studying in order to reach as high an academic education as possible. For the theory is, the higher his grades are, the more chances he has of getting a very good job with a good pay packet as a reward for his dedication.

SUMMARY OF THE ARIES/PIG CHARACTERISTICS AND BEHAVIOR:

☺ Generous, loyal, good natured, optimistic, industrious, calm, friendly, tolerant.

☹ Anxious, quick-tempered, excessive, naïve, easily bored, demanding, stubborn.

IF THIS CHILD IS MISBEHAVING:

The Pig year is accepted as the most mature, so treat this child with that philosophy. From the start only accept his best. And he will respond with that demand as he's naturally intelligent and wanting to be honest in his behaviours. He loves to negotiate, so allow this ability to develop as it will help him in his future life. He is usually well-tempered, generous, loyal and helpful. Keep him interested and focused on his own studies, rather than going around helping everyone else. As a negative, he can be excessive, both in his emotions and behaviours and has a quick temper. He will tease others, but dislikes it when he's made to look silly. His naivety may lead him to be gullible, in which case he will try to get back at his tormentors in the best of underhand ways. His advantage is that he is psychic and can anticipate other peoples' reactions, which he can use for his own benefits.

This merger of birth signs makes for a child who can go to extremes in his activities. Therefore a firm hand is recommended, with lots of one-to-one talks at eye level. This child will not take well to being told what to do and could respond aggressively to criticism. Equally he hates being threatened, so any comments should be offered thoughtfully and casually. He is touchy, so use this as a weapon to keep him in his place, or else he will try to rule the home. He might use his fierce temper to play judge and jury. But the best is to get him to use his energies to help around the home and to work hard at school. However, because of his fondness of decadence, watch out that he doesn't over indulge in his love to eat sweets or fatty foods when he is frustrated or feeling vulnerable. This child is able to do very well when motivated with kindness. But he will resent being blamed for something he's not responsible for, so be prepared to have an angry youth if he feels misunderstood. Keep him busy with his school studies and reward him for his successes.

FAMOUS ARIES/PIG PERSONALITIES

Roberto Casadesus (7 April 1899): A French pianist and composer. He was the most prominent member of a famous musical family. After World War II he went to the USA where he founded the Fontainebleau music school with his wife in Rhode Island. His life story portrays the elements of the Aries/Pig personality.

Tennessee William (26 March 1911): An American Pulitzer Prize playwright. After many years in obscurity he became famous with his play, The Glass Menagerie, which received great acclaim, forever changing his life and fortunes. Two years later, A Streetcar Named Desire opened, surpassing his previous success and cementing his status as one of the country's best playwrights. Sadly in the 1960s his work started to receive poor reviews and he increasingly turned to alcohol and drugs as coping mechanisms. But he never fully escaped his demons. His life story makes for interesting reading to describe the Aries/Pig's excessive personality.

Charles F. Brush III (3 April 1923): An American archaeologist. He led archaeological expeditions around the world before turning to more daring feats including climbing volcanoes and scaling some of the highest mountain summits. He served as president of the Explorers Club, gaining notoriety by allowing women to join this elite group. He was seen as an eccentric personality, but he could afford it as he had inherited a vast fortune from his family.

Mahmoud Abbas (26 March 1935): President of the Palestinian National Authority. He has been trying to bring peace to Israel since he took office in 2004. He has had to overcome many political problems with his own people e.g. The Hamas military group, which is an active terror organization opposed to any peaceful solution with Israel.

Abelardo Castillo (27 March 1935): an Argentine writer, novelist and essayist. He practiced amateur boxing in his youth. He also directed the literary magazine El Escarabajo de Oro (the Golden Beetle.) He is well regarded in the field of Latin American literature. In 2014 he won the Diamond Konex Award as the best writer in the last decade in Argentina.

Dudley Moore (19 April 1935): An English award-winning actor, comedian and composer. He started out as a child musical prodigy and was a renowned performer. As a comedic actor, he astonished fans all over the world with his talents and abilities, which brought him great acclaim and success. In addition to acting, he continued to work as a composer and pianist, writing scores for a number of films and giving piano concerts. In 2001 he was awarded a CBE for his services to entertainment.

Sir Elton John (25 March 1947): An English, singer, song writer, composer and pianist. In his five-decade career he has sold more than 300 million records, making him one of the best-selling music artists in the world. He has also found success on Broadway, composing the music score for the Tony award-winning hit, Billy Elliot. He was inducted into the Rock and Roll Hall of Fame in 1994 and was knighted in 1998.

Alain Connes (1 April 1947): A French mathematician and currently a Distinguished Professor at Ohio State University. He is known for Noncommutative Geometry and has won many accolades for his innovative work. As an inspirational and energetic lecturer, he has applied his work to the areas of mathematics and theoretical physics, including number theory, differential geometry and particle physics. He is the prototype for the active but wise Aries/Pig personality.

Robert Kiyosaki (5 April 1947): An American investor, business man, and author of popular self-help books. He is also a motivational speaker, financial literacy activist and financial commentator. He has written 15 books with sales of over 26 million copies. And because of his success he now wants to help others do the same.

Hasnat Khan (1 April 1959): A British Pakistani heart and lung surgeon. He had a two-year relationship with Diana, Princess of Wales. Their romance is the subject of the book Diana: Her Last Love, and its film adaptation, 'Diana' was released in 2013, despite Khan's disapproval. His future plan is to establish free cardiac health services for the poor in Badlot, Pakistan. As a true Aries/Pig, he wants to share his knowledge and abilities with the rest of the world to bring happiness to those around him.

Andrew Bailey (30 March 1959): An English executive Director of the Bank of England from 2004 to 2011. He is now serving as the Deputy Governor for the Prudential Regulation Department, keeping an eye on the expenses. He is a good prototype for an Aries/Pig personality.

David Coulthard (27 March 1971): A British former Formula One racing driver turned presenter, commentator and journalist. In his Formula One career, he won 13 Grand Prix titles, took 12 pole positions, set 18 fastest laps and scored 535 World Championship points. In 2010 he was awarded an MBE for his services to motor racing. He is daring, but at the same time a cautious Aries/Pig. But most of all he is charming, and very well informed.

David Tennant (18 April 1971): A Scottish actor, famous for his role in the Doctor Who TV series. His love life is as interesting as his acting career, as it shows all the traits of an Aries/Pig's personality; having a zest for new experiences in his romantic roles.

Toni Elias (16 April 1983): A Spanish motorbike rider. The first World Champion of the Moto 2 category. He has raced in all four levels of Grand Prix motorcycle racing. Now he is riding for the Super Bike class for the Red Devils Roma. He is always trying to improve his riding style, as his aim is to win as many races as possible. For as a true Aries/Pig he hates to lose. His aim is to use all his experience to take calculated risks as an Aries, and learn from his falls as a true Pig.

ACKNOWLEDGMENTS

To my parents who worked to turn a selfish semi-wild youth into an attentive student. My kind-hearted mother (Sagittarius/Goat) protected me from myself, and my father (Scorpio/Dragon) with his determined personality to self-improve and see to it that his family prospered at all costs.

To the teachers who had a huge influence in my personal development as a free-thinking individualist; Brother Taylor, Brother Dougherty and Brother Foley. And though long dead, I am beholden to them for their efforts to get me to calm down to realize my potential.

To my three children Nicole, Suzanne and Jacey for living my theory of family genetics and constellations. They represent the very essence of my family's history. For each has faced life as a strong individual, conquered it, and then turned to help others.

To Cindy Draughon who edited my first draft and was brave enough to tell me to cut down my lengthy explanations and double telling of the same theme. As my book doctor par excellence, I am indebted to you.

To Teresa Lluansi and Amparo Shalome for their guidance and prayers, and which allowed me to turn an 11-year hobby into reality.

To the many parents who answered my call to give feedback on what I had written about their children. Some found the information confrontational, but thankfully agreed I was right in my descriptions of their offspring and their relationship with them.

And finally, to every one of my 'Thursday family.' Over the many years we have been meeting your words have inspired and guided me. Your compassion, honesty, support and friendship is without bounds and has allowed me to truly understand the meaning of fellowship.

My thanks and gratitude to you all.